NEW DIRECTIONS FOR CHILD DEVELOPMENT

William Damon, *Brown University*
EDITOR-IN-CHIEF

The Emergence of Core Domains of Thought: Children's Reasoning About Physical, Psychological, and Biological Phenomena

Henry M. Wellman
University of Michigan

Kayoko Inagaki
Chiba University, Japan

EDITORS

Number 75, Spring 1997

JOSSEY-BASS PUBLISHERS
San Francisco

THE EMERGENCE OF CORE DOMAINS OF THOUGHT: CHILDREN'S REASONING
ABOUT PHYSICAL, PSYCHOLOGICAL, AND BIOLOGICAL PHENOMENA
Henry M. Wellman, Kayoko Inagaki (eds.)
New Directions for Child Development, no. 75
William Damon, Editor-in-Chief

Microfilm copies of issues and articles are available in 16mm and 35mm,
as well as microfiche in 105mm, through University Microfilms Inc., 300
North Zeeb Road, Ann Arbor, Michigan 48106-1346.

ISSN 0195-2269   ISBN 0-7879-9844-3

NEW DIRECTIONS FOR CHILD DEVELOPMENT is part of The Jossey-Bass
Education Series and is published quarterly by Jossey-Bass Inc., Publishers,
350 Sansome Street, San Francisco, California 94104-1342. Periodicals
postage paid at San Francisco, California, and at additional mailing
offices. POSTMASTER: Send address changes to New Directions for Child
Development, Jossey-Bass Inc., Publishers, 350 Sansome Street, San Francisco, California 94104-1342.

New Directions for Child Development® is indexed in Biosciences Information Service, Current Index to Journals in Education (ERIC), Psychological Abstracts, and Sociological Abstracts.

SUBSCRIPTIONS cost $65.00 for individuals and $105.00 for institutions,
agencies, and libraries.

EDITORIAL CORRESPONDENCE should be sent to the Editor-in-Chief,
William Damon, Department of Education, Box 1938, Brown University,
Providence, Rhode Island 02912.

Cover photograph by Wernher Krutein/PHOTOVAULT © 1990.

Jossey-Bass Web address: http://www.josseybass.com

 Manufactured in the United States of America on Lyons Falls Turin
Book. This paper is acid-free and 100 percent totally chlorine-free.

CONTENTS

EDITORS' NOTES 1
Henry M. Wellman, Kayoko Inagaki

1. Young Children's Psychological, Physical, and 7
Biological Explanations
Henry M. Wellman, Anne K. Hickling, Carolyn A. Schult
Preschoolers appropriately use three different reasoning systems in their
explanations of everyday phenomena, especially human behavior.

2. Emerging Distinctions Between Naive Biology and 27
Naive Psychology
Kayoko Inagaki
Psychological and biological reasoning are intertwined yet differentiated in
preschoolers' understandings of bodily processes and events.

3. Are Children with Autism Superior at Folk Physics? 45
Simon Baron-Cohen
Children with autism show superiority in folk physics but deficits in folk
psychology.

4. Domain Specificity and Everyday Biological, Physical, 55
and Psychological Thinking in Normal, Autistic, and
Deaf Children
Candida C. Peterson, Michael Siegal
Conversational differences in the language young children hear accounts for
their distinctive patterns of understanding biological, physical, and psychological phenomena.

5. Commentary: Core Domains of Thought, Innate Constraints, 71
and Sociocultural Contexts
Giyoo Hatano
Early development of core domains of thought is guided by both innate and
sociocultural constraints.

INDEX 79

EDITORS' NOTES

What do children know about the world—about friends, families, pets, trees, rocks, clouds, bicycles, television, birth, death, love, and Santa Claus? Their concepts and beliefs about these and other phenomena constitute their knowledge systems and define their worldview. These conceptions are both the products and the containers of childhood cognition and development.

To gain insight into children's developing understanding of the world, a growing number of studies have addressed children's knowledge about everyday physical, biological, and psychological phenomena. These seem to be three major domains of understanding for human beings, in that they encompass much of the reality with which all people—children and adults—interact. They include persons and their mental life, plants and animals and their attempts for survival, and physical objects and their movements.

Human beings are a notably social species: we communicate, cooperate, and collude. We also create and use artifacts. Like all species, we inhabit ecological niches in a biophysical world, and our bodies must be fed and kept healthy. Acquiring knowledge about psychological, physical, and biological phenomena is thus a crucial part of our cognitive development. Biological, physical, and psychological phenomena and reasoning are not only important but also, arguably, separable. Languages and cultures worldwide make various distinctions between animate and inanimate, between subject and object, and between psychological entities, living things, and physical objects. Consider our opening examples: friends, families, love, and even Santa Claus are in some ways similar in their social-psychological nature or explanation; pets, trees, birth, and death are all biological phenomena; rocks, clouds, and bicycles are (in our culture at least) all distinctly physical objects or systems.

If we assume that adults possess differentiated understandings of psychological, biological, and physical phenomena, then several questions arise about human cognitive development. Do children distinguish between these three domains of thought? If so, when do they do so—late in childhood, so that these conceptions represent the culmination of knowledge acquisition, or early in life, so that these distinctions set a basic infrastructure for learning and development? Piaget, in his early studies (1929), argued for late differentiation. He claimed that until the elementary school years children are fundamentally confused about these three knowledge systems. Young children, according to Piaget, are confused about what sorts of things are alive or not; about what things are natural, artifactual, or merely mental; about causal reasoning in general and thus about differences in biological, physical, and psychological causes and explanations; and about which sorts of causal-explanatory reasonings apply to which sorts of entities and phenomena. Relatedly, discussions of childhood socialization leading to the acquisition of varied

1

folk theories—especially culturally distinctive folk theories concerning personhood, life, plants and animals, and the physical surround of earth, sun, stars, and storms—often assume a prolonged, tutored acquisition of societally sanctioned beliefs and expertise.

However, recently an increasing number of scholars have argued that important understandings of these three domains develop early in life and are hence basic (for example, see Astington, Harris, and Olson 1988; Atran, 1990; Spelke, 1994; Wellman and Gelman, 1992). All the chapters in this sourcebook provide evidence of impressive early understandings. Moreover, in doing so they consider a wide range of children from the United States, Japan, Britain, and Australia, including normal, autistic, retarded, and deaf individuals. This focus on early knowledge and understanding is by design; the authors of this sourcebook were chosen because they are major contributors to our increasingly international understanding of early cognitive development (for example, see Wellman, 1990; Hatano and Inagaki, 1994; Baron-Cohen, 1995; Peterson and Siegal, 1995).

In this sourcebook we advance and articulate a variety of "early competence" positions regarding cognitive development. We do so by considering the nature, timing, and development of children's conceptions of basic psychological, biological, and physical phenomena. Of course, no one contends that the development of knowledge in these domains ends in early childhood. Much knowledge develops, on many fronts, beyond those conceptions that are the focus of this sourcebook. But all of the authors of this sourcebook believe that later cognitive development rests on and makes use of the earlier developments discussed here.

Interestingly, despite the increasing number of studies addressing these topics, seldom have researchers focused on making comparisons across these three modes of thinking—psychological versus physical versus biological reasoning. For the most part, recent studies have dealt with a single mode of thinking. For example, research on children's understandings of the physical world has examined infants' understanding of object permanence and physical forces (for example, Spelke, 1994; Baillargeon, Kotovsky, and Needham, 1995) and older children's understanding of physical causality (for example, Bullock, Gelman, and Baillargeon, 1982; Shultz, 1982). Research on children's naive psychological understandings, or their "theory of mind," has examined children's understanding of beliefs, emotions, and belief-desire reasoning (for example, see Wellman, 1990; Harris, 1989; Perner, 1991). Research on children's understandings of biological phenomena has focused on their conceptions of life (Carey, 1985), growth (Rosengren, Gelman, Kalish, and McCormick, 1991), and inheritance (Keil, 1989).

A new direction, represented by all the chapters in this sourcebook, is to compare cognitive functions across these three domains of understanding. If they are indeed distinctive domains of thought, then they should yield uneven profiles of competence (especially, perhaps, in special populations of children); they should be served by different cognitive mechanisms or reasoning systems, at some level of analysis; and children should become adept at differentiating between them, at least at some point in their development and for certain sorts of problems. Understanding the extent to which the physical, biological, and psychological worlds form the basis of core domains of thought requires researchers to address these issues. The contributors to this sourcebook have tackled just this task.

Although the authors all assume "early competence," they differ in their views concerning the nature of the development of core domains of thought. One possibility is that these core domains originate in certain innate conceptions or preferences but have to be gradually differentiated one from the other. This has been argued clearly and persuasively, for example, by Susan Carey concerning the relationship between biological and psychological reasoning. In an earlier work, Carey (1985) argued that initially children view phenomena such as eating, gender, growth, and illness—phenomena that are predominantly biological for adults—as psychological or social in nature. For example, she argued that eating is first understood in terms of social conventions about mealtimes and the identification of particular foods as "good" or "bad," rather than in terms of ingestion and digestion of essential nutrients. Similarly, she argued that sexual differences are first understood in terms of social signals (such as dress) and psychological states (such as aggressiveness or caring) rather than in terms of biological differences and reproductive function. Recently (1995) she lowered her estimate of the age at which biology is differentiated from psychology, from age ten to age six or seven, but she still maintains that children younger than six do not distinguish biological phenomena from psychological ones in their reasoning and understanding. Directly comparing young children's biological reasoning versus their psychological reasoning about various phenomena is thus essential to prove the validity of this hypothesis and to address the larger issue of the differentiation of domains of thought.

Chapter Two, by Kayoko Inagaki, directly addresses this question. Inagaki concludes that preschoolers do distinguish biological phenomena from psychological ones in their causal reasoning, although their reasoning about biological phenomena is sometimes influenced by psychological conceptions and considerations as well. Chapter One, by Henry Wellman, Anne Hickling, and Carolyn Schult, and Chapter Four, by Candida Peterson and Michael Siegazl, also take up the issue of differentiation, using tasks from all three of these distinctive domains.

A different, though related, possibility is that naive understandings of psychological, biological, and physical phenomena are similar at a general level of analysis, in that they all represent everyday folk theories. While they are thus similar in certain ways (even for young children), these understandings may represent profoundly different everyday theories that rest on different theoretical constructs and invoke very different explanatory devices. For example, physical objects are typically construed in terms of mass, center of gravity, and solidity and require causal or explanatory reasoning in terms of contact, momentum, and trajectories. By contrast, psychological understanding focuses on mental states such as emotions, dreams, and ideas and the reasons, motives, and intentions that produce them. Biological understanding may focus on everyday constructs such as essences and innate potential (the "stuff" that makes horses horses and not zebras, even if one were to paint a white horse with black stripes), and it utilizes causes or explanations such as animateness, growth, and reproduction.

If these three domains of thought do reflect distinctive everyday theories, then children's explanations of specific biological, physical, and psychological phenomena should be quite different. Theories, at their hearts, provide causal-explanatory reasoning systems (Carey, 1985; Laudan, 1977; Wellman, 1990). Chapter One, by Henry Wellman, Anne Hickling, and Carolyn Schult, takes up young children's explanations of contrasting phenomena and uses them to argue for a theory-type view of biological, psychological, and physical domains of thought. The authors conclude that "children evidence at least three basic everyday reasoning systems as early as two years of age—physical and psychological reasoning surely, and even biological reasoning in a rudimentary form."

Another view concerning the nature of these domains is that thinking about physical versus psychological versus biological phenomena is represented in different cognitive modules or brain systems. For example, humans have visual systems that present us with a world filled with color, but we do not have an echolocation system (like bats) to present us with a similarly rich sonic world. Similarly, we may have evolved special cognitive modules that allow us to think in special ways about inanimate objects, living organisms, or persons—for example, brain systems that process information about faces and make faces especially interesting even to infants; systems that make biological movements easily encoded and represented; even, perhaps, special systems that construe persons predominantly in terms of their internal intentions rather than their external appearance. For example, a study of functional neurological imaging (Fletcher and others, 1995) found that thoughtful consideration of a sequence of intentional actions activated a different area of the brain than did consideration of a physical sequence of events. Such findings lead to the general possibility that a variety of content-specific mental modules exist (and might be impaired in some individuals). More specifically, these considerations have led to the specific proposal that autistic individuals are impaired in the development of normal brain systems supporting naive psychological reasoning and understanding. In Chapter Three, Simon Baron-Cohen argues along these lines and discusses his large and intriguing research program addressing core domains of thought—psychological versus nonpsychological understandings—with autistic individuals. Going beyond his earlier studies, which revealed characteristic profiles of performance on psychological reasoning tasks for autistic, normal, and retarded individuals, he provides new data suggesting that autistic individuals may have "superior folk physics alongside impaired folk psychology."

Candida Peterson and Michael Siegal follow in Baron-Cohen's footsteps in Chapter Four, addressing psychological, physical, and even biological understandings in autistic individuals. Their data mimic Baron-Cohen's in showing a divergence between psychological and physical understandings in autistic individuals, and hence they provide clear evidence for important differences between these domains of thought. In addition, however, Peterson and Siegal present evidence about deaf individuals' reasoning on these problems and argue for a different sort of account of the nature of impairments in psychological reasoning. According to their data, deaf individuals who were raised by hearing parents (and thus without fluent conversational interaction in sign language) show deficits in psychological reasoning that look much like those of autistics. Deaf individuals who have grown up in a family with a fluent signer do not show such deficits. Because deafness does not have the same neurological basis presumed for autism, their data suggest a possibility that a theory of mind is acquired through conversational experiences. Peterson and Siegal argue that early, conversational deficits and experiences are primarily important for the development of naive psychological understandings. Although they do not deny that these distinct domains have some innate bases, they allude to the possibility of characterizing all these domains as being based on the gaining of expertise.

Together, the first four chapters of this sourcebook vigorously advance our understanding of cognitive development by directly comparing children's understanding of and reasoning about the psychological, biological, and physical worlds in which they live. They describe and elaborate on the three major theoretical positions that currently compete to explain cognitive development—theory-theory, modular, and experiential accounts of early knowledge acquisition (Wellman and Gelman, forthcoming). These chapters set the stage for further research and theory, and they set the stage for the insightful commentary on these issues offered by Giyoo Hatano in Chapter Five. Hatano places the preceding chapters in a larger perspective, raising challenges for further research on this important new direction in understanding children's thinking and cognitive development.

Henry M. Wellman
Kayoko Inagaki
Editors

References

Astington, J. W., Harris, P. L., and Olson, D. R. *Developing Theories of Mind.* New York: Cambridge University Press, 1988.
Atran, S. *Cognitive Foundations of Natural History.* Cambridge, England: Cambridge University Press, 1990.
Baillargeon, R., Kotovsky, L., and Needham, A. "The Acquisition of Physical Knowledge in Infancy." In D. Sperber, D. Premack, and A. J. Premack (eds.), *Causal Cognition: A Multidisciplinary Debate.* New York: Oxford University Press, 1995.

Baron-Cohen, S. *Mindblindness: An Essay on Autism and Theory of Mind.* Cambridge, Mass.: MIT Press, 1995.

Bullock, M., Gelman, R., and Baillargeon, R. "The Development of Causal Reasoning." In W. J. Friedman (ed.), *The Developmental Psychology of Time.* Orlando: Academic Press, 1982.

Carey, S. *Conceptual Change in Childhood.* Cambridge, Mass.: MIT Press, 1985.

Carey, S. "On the Origin of Causal Understanding." In D. Sperber, D. Premack, and A. J. Premack (eds.), *Causal Cognition: A Multi-disciplinary Debate.* New York: Oxford University Press, 1995.

Fletcher, P. C., and others. "Other Minds in the Brain: A Functional Imaging Study of 'Theory of Mind' in Story Comprehension." *Cognition,* 1995, *57,* 109–128.

Harris, P. L. *Children and Emotion.* Oxford, England: Blackwell, 1989.

Hatano, G., and Inagaki, K. "Young Children's Naive Theory of Biology." *Cognition,* 1994, *50,* 171–188.

Keil, F. C. *Concepts, Kinds, and Cognitive Development.* Cambridge, Mass.: MIT Press, 1989.

Laudan, L. *Progress and Its Problems: Towards a Theory of Scientific Growth.* Berkeley: University of California Press, 1977.

Perner, J. *Understanding the Representational Mind.* Cambridge, Mass.: MIT Press, 1991.

Peterson, C. C., and Siegal, M. "Deafness, Conversation and Theory of Mind." *Journal of Child Psychology and Psychiatry,* 1995, *36,* 459–474.

Piaget, J. *The Child's Conception of the World.* New York: Routledge, 1929.

Rosengren, K. S., Gelman, S. A., Kalish, C. W., and McCormick, M. "As Time Goes By: Children's Early Understanding of Growth in Animals." *Child Development,* 1991, *62,* 1302–1320.

Shultz, T. R. *Rules of Causal Attribution.* Monographs of the Society for Research in Child Development, no. 194. Chicago: University of Chicago Press, 1982.

Spelke, E. S. "Initial Knowledge: Six Suggestions." *Cognition,* 1994, *50,* 431–455.

Wellman, H. M. *The Child's Theory of Mind.* Cambridge, Mass.: MIT Press, 1990.

Wellman, H. M., and Gelman, S. A. "Cognitive Development: Foundational Theories of Core Domains." *Annual Review of Psychology,* 1992, *43,* 337–375.

Wellman, H. M., and Gelman, S. A. "Knowledge Acquisition in Foundational Domains." In W. Damon (ed.), *Handbook of Child Psychology* (5th ed.), Vol. 2 (D. Kuhn and R. Siegler, eds.): *Cognition, Perception and Language.* New York: Wiley, forthcoming.

HENRY M. WELLMAN *is professor in the Department of Psychology and research scientist at the Center for Human Growth and Development at the University of Michigan, Ann Arbor.*

KAYOKO INAGAKI *is professor of education at Chiba University, Japan.*

Laboratory and natural language analyses of two-, three-, and four-year-olds' explanations of human behavior show them appropriately distinguishing between psychological, physical, and biological reasoning.

Young Children's Psychological, Physical, and Biological Explanations

Henry M. Wellman, Anne K. Hickling, Carolyn A. Schult

When we explain something, we make sense of it within some framework or another. Beyond such general descriptions, defining what we mean by an explanation is not a simple matter. Understanding complex psychological constructs of this sort requires more a theory than a straightforward definition. But, minimally, explanations capture our search for and beliefs about what connects with what and what accounts for what. Moreover, explanations range over many phenomena and partake of many reasoning systems. Imagine someone whose body is shaking all over. Adults in our society might believe that the person is shaking with fear (a psychological reason), shivering with a fever (a biological cause), or even shaking from an earthquake tremor (a physical explanation). In this chapter we claim that early in life children develop three distinctive causal-explanatory reasoning systems:

1. A naive psychology (a theory of mind) that involves construing human action in terms of actors' internal mental states
2. A naive physics—an early understanding of mechanical or material phenomena, such as objects colliding, falling, or having mass
3. A naive biology—an early understanding of everyday physiological states and processes, such as illness, birth, growth, and death.

Preparation of this chapter and conduct of the research reported here was supported by grant HD-22149 from the National Institute of Child Health and Human Development to Henry Wellman and a Rackham Predoctoral Fellowship from the Graduate School of the University of Michigan to Anne Hickling.

7

A variety of research already supports such a claim (Wellman and Gelman, 1992, forthcoming). Three- and four-year-olds understand that animals and plants but not inanimate objects grow and heal (Backscheider, Shatz, and Gelman, 1993; Inagaki and Hatano, 1996; Rosengren, Gelman, Kalish, and McCormick, 1991); that natural phenomena such as clouds, stars, and animals have natural causes rather than artificial ones (Gelman and Kremer, 1991); that persons but not dolls or rocks can think, remember, feel happy, and see (Gelman, Spelke, and Meck, 1983; Johnson and Wellman, 1982); and that thoughts are mental and nonmaterial whereas physical entities such as balls and dogs are tangible and material (Wellman and Estes, 1986). Some of these distinctions may constrain conceptual understandings from a very early age indeed; even infants appropriately distinguish between animate and inanimate entities and their movements (Legerstee, 1992; Spelke, Phillips, and Woodward, 1995). Piaget (1929), among others, claimed that children initially confuse together these forms of reasoning, which are fundamentally distinct in adults' thoughts, resulting in childhood animism, artificialism, and realism. But many current studies (such as those just cited) argue that even quite young children may reason about psychological, biological, and physical phenomena differently and appropriately.

This emerging research is incomplete, however. As noted in the Editors' Notes, rarely have investigators looked at children's reasoning comparatively, across these three topics or domains of thinking. If naive psychology, physics, and biology constitute contrasting reasoning systems, then children must come to differentiate and coordinate them in revealing fashions. Furthermore, contemporary research has typically examined children's judgments and predictions—whether rabbits can heal or grow, what actions will stem from a character's beliefs and desires. Much less is known about children's explanations. Yet, writers have often called these three reasoning systems naive theories (for example, see Wellman and Gelman, 1992), thereby emphasizing their presumed status as *explanatory* knowledge systems. If naive psychology, physics, and biology constitute developing causal-explanatory reasoning systems, then this should be especially important for, and be especially revealed by, children's explanations.

For the last few years, therefore, we have been researching children's explanations of psychological, biological, and physical phenomena. We have examined a range of topics and events, but in this chapter we concentrate on children's explanation of human movements and actions.

Explanations of Human Behavior

Both theoretical and methodological reasons make children's explanations of human movements an important and revealing topic. Methodologically, if the aim is to compare children's psychological, physical, and biological reasoning, human beings and human movement are the primary phenomena where all three explanations appropriately apply. Recall the example of the person who is shaking all over. Humans are not only psychological entities motivated by mental processes, they are also physical bodies subject to objectlike movements and biological organisms subject to physiological forces and movements. Thus, studying children's explanations of human movements provides a focus for comparing their reasoning across a variety of explanatory systems.

Theoretically, assume for the moment that young children do possess several different explanatory reasoning systems—say, psychological, physical, and biological ones. Then how do children coordinate the different sorts of entities to be explained with the distinctive principles or constructs that may be used to explain them? One obvious possibility is that children apply each reasoning system to every sort of entity. This possibility provides a plausible core to Piaget's varied claims about animism, realism, and artificialism. Children might very well use physical, biological, or psychological explanations indiscriminately for a very wide range of phenomena, at least at some early point in their cognitive development. The opposite possibility is also plausible. That is, each reasoning system could have its own proprietary entities, at least early in a child's development. Thus, for young children mental-psychological explanations might apply always and solely to people, mechanical-physical explanations always and solely to inanimate physical objects, and biological explanations always and solely to nonhuman living things. Carey and Spelke (1994), among others, argue for this entity-based possibility—entities and explanations go together, to begin with, in certain tightly woven ways. Targeting human beings and human movements provides a way to test these alternative proposals.

We know from some earlier work of our own that when asked to explain simple human actions (for example, "Jane is looking for her kitten under the piano, why is she doing that?") or simple human reactions ("Joe went to school today and saw they were having grape juice for snack. Boy was he surprised. Why is Joe so surprised?"), three- and four-year-olds, like adults, typically provide psychological explanations (Bartsch and Wellman, 1989; Wellman and Banerjee, 1991). Predominantly, children and adults explain these actions and reactions in terms of the actors' beliefs and desires ("She wants to find her kitten" or "He thought they'd have orange juice, not grape juice, for snack"). But these studies focused on a limited range of human acts; biological movements or reactions (feverish shaking) and physical, objectlike movements were not included. A few prior studies have included these sorts of human movements, and they suggest that young children might make some telling errors in applying different reasoning systems to human behavior. Shultz, Wells, and Sardo (1980) asked preschool children to judge reflex and intended behaviors. Until five years of age children judged *both* these types of behaviors to be "on purpose." Relatedly, Smith (1978) showed four-, five-, and six-year-olds videotapes of an actor engaging in voluntary acts (such as chewing something, doing arm exercises) *or* undergoing reflex reactions (yawning, saying "Ow" when poked with a stick in the ribs) *or* experiencing objectlike movement (having an arm snagged and raised by the hook of an umbrella, being pushed across the room like a large box). Children were asked whether the actor had been "trying" to do what she did, whether she had been "surprised" at what she did, and whether she had "wanted" to do what she did. Not until five years did children distinguish reflexes and objectlike movements from intentional (that is, psychologically based) behavior: "Four-year-olds tended to regard all acts/movements and their effects as intentional. Object-like movements and involuntary acts as well as voluntary acts were generally judged intentional" (p. 741).

Our Recent Studies of Children's Explanations

For several reasons we felt that earlier research might not have captured children's understandings adequately. Therefore, in a series of studies (Schult and Wellman, forthcoming) we solicited explanations from three- and four-year-olds of a variety of human actions and movements with a psychological, biological, or physical impetus. Exhibit 1.1 presents some of the situations we used. Voluntary actions that actors perform because they want to are prototypical psychologically caused movements (for example, a person pours milk on her cereal). Psychological explanations of such acts often stress the subject's beliefs or desires—"he wanted milk on his cereal" or "he thinks cereal is better with milk than dry." Mistakes; physical, objectlike movements; and biological movements contrast with such intended actions. For example, mistakes are unintended—something happens that is not a result or fulfillment of the subject's desires. Although unintended, mistakes require psychological explanations just as intended actions do. For adults, at least, mistakes are explained by an appeal to psychological causes such as beliefs and desires—"he didn't know the pitcher had orange juice," or "he thought it had milk." Biological human behaviors, such as reflexes, or physical, objectlike movements, such as being blown along by the wind, are like mistakes in their being unintended and also in that they often go counter to a person's desires. Yet, for adults these sorts of behaviors require nonpsychological construal and explanation; their explanations lie in the domains of physical and biological forces and processes.

In several studies three- and four-year-olds each heard four to six stories of the sort in Exhibit 1.1, presented with the aid of several line drawings. A critical comparison to be made in these studies concerned children's responses to mistakes versus their responses to physical and biological movements. As in Exhibit 1.1, in those three types of stories the protagonist's desire was similarly thwarted; nevertheless, for adults at least the explanations for these three actions or movements should be quite different. The stories were presented, the outcomes were noted, and the children were asked to explain what had happened. "Why did [that outcome] happen? Why did [the protagonist] do that?" For example, "Why did Jimmy pour orange juice on his cereal?"

Children's explanations ranged over a variety of topics and processes, but they were easily and reliably coded into the following categories:

Exhibit 1.1. Sample Items for Eliciting Explanations from Preschoolers

Intended action

It's time for breakfast, so Jimmy gets the cereal out of the cupboard. Now Jimmy has an idea. He wants to pour milk on his cereal. Jimmy takes a pitcher out of the refrigerator and pours it on his cereal. He pours milk on his cereal.

Mistake

It's time for breakfast, so Jimmy gets the cereal out of the cupboard. Now Jimmy has an idea. He wants to pour milk on his cereal. Jimmy takes a pitcher out of the refrigerator and pours it on his cereal. He pours orange juice on his cereal.

Biological

Robin is climbing a tree in her backyard. She's hanging from a branch, not touching the ground. Now she has an idea. She wants to hang on that branch forever and never let go. Robin drops to the ground.

Physical

Bobby is playing in his bedroom. He climbs on top of his stool. Now he has an idea. He wants to step off the stool and float in the air, up off the floor. Bobby steps off the stool and comes right down to the floor.

Source: Adapted from Schult and Wellman, forthcoming.

- *Psychological explanations:* statements that referred to the character's mental states, such as his or her desires, preferences, beliefs, and emotions. "He wanted to get down." "She just didn't know it was ketchup." "He thought it was milk."
- *Physical explanations:* statements that appealed to or implied physical forces, such as gravity or the wind, or statements declaring the need for some other mechanism for the action to be carried out. "He's too heavy to float in the sky." "Gravity pulls him down." "Planes can fly and people can't, 'cause they don't have wings."
- *Biological explanations:* statements that referred to states of the body, such as fatigue or pain, or to biological processes, such as growth, health, blood, and germs. "He gets tired and has to sleep again." "His arms got hurting." "You have to grow bigger."
- *Other:* statements that reiterated the story, said "don't know," or were uninterpretable.

Figure 1.1 shows how children in a study comparing three- and four-year-olds explained each story type. As the figure makes clear, far from regarding all these human movements and actions as being due to the actors' desires, beliefs, and intentions, young children were appropriately selective as to the kinds of actions that deserved a psychological explanation. For four-year-olds, mistakes, like voluntary acts, received psychological explanations, although these acts differed in whether the characters' desires were achieved. Yet, in

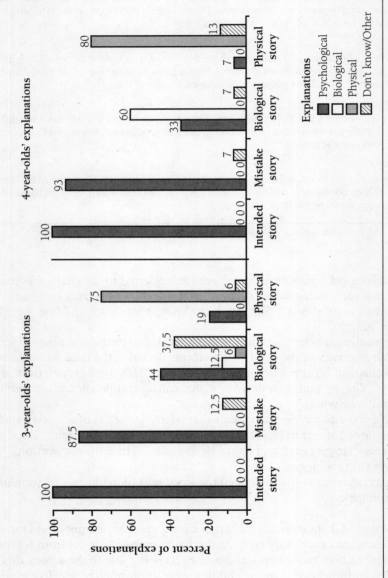

Figure 1.1. Explanations for Intended, Mistaken, Biological, and Physical Movements or Events

Source: Adapted from Schult and Wellman, forthcoming.

contrast to mistakes, physical, objectlike movements received largely physical explanations, and organic or biologically based movements received largely biological explanations. Even three-year-olds mostly fit this pattern, at least in comparing psychologically caused versus physically caused movements or events.

Note how flexible and appropriate the children's explanations were. Although not shown in Exhibit 1.1, each physical and biological item was typically paired with an intended item focusing on the same behavioral occurrence. For example, coming down from a stool because of gravity was paired with coming down because the character wanted to. Children explained the same surface acts differently and appropriately. Moreover, items were carefully constructed so that surface features of the movements and situations to be explained could not simply elicit correct explanations. For example, the "Mistake" scenario in Exhibit 1.1 actually focuses on eating breakfast, a potentially biological activity. Children explained this scenario appropriately, in psychological terms, and not simply by recruiting various associated "biological" terms such as hunger, food, or energy. Similarly, both the biological and the physical items in Exhibit 1.1 involved coming down to the ground from a height, but children explained these movements differently. Overall, children's explanations gave no evidence that they might simply be matching associated terms to the surface phenomena described in the scenarios (for example, eating inspiring mention of growth or nutrition, and dropping or falling inspiring mention of gravity or weight). Instead, children's explanations appropriately targeted the deeper causal event—the everyday psychological, biological, and physical forces that adults also believe are at play in such scenarios.

In an additional study we wished to explore children's reasoning about a larger array of items. Here we began by asking children to determine whether some desired action could occur. Three different types of desired actions were contrasted, as shown in Exhibit 1.2. In the case of simple, voluntary actions like lying down or jumping, the desire or intention generally results in the action, in a straightforward manner—if you want to perform the action, you can do it. For physically or biologically impossible actions, however, like floating in the air without support or never experiencing pain, psychological motivation simply cannot bring about the desired action or result, because other forces—physical and biological constraints—are also at work. In this study three-year-olds and four-year-olds were presented with nine scenarios of the sort shown in Exhibit 1.2. After each scenario was described, the child was asked if the character could do the desired action: "Can he do that?" Then the children were asked to explain their judgments: "Why?" or "Why not?"

There were only small and insignificant differences between the three- and four-year-olds in their judgments. When asked about the voluntary items, the four-year-olds judged 93 percent of the time that, yes, the character could do that (the three-year-olds did so 82 percent of the time). When asked about the physically impossible items, the four-year-olds judged 90 percent of the time that, no, the character could *not* do that (the three-year-olds judged so 83

Exhibit 1.2. Explanations for Intended, Mistaken, Biological, and Physical Movements or Events

Voluntary actions, possible

Fred is in his room standing with his feet on the floor. He's been standing up a long time. Now he wants to have it different, and that's OK with his mom. He wants to stop standing up and lie down on his bed.

Cathy has been sitting outside on a bench for a long time. She's been sitting quietly watching the trees. Now she wants something different, and it's OK with her mom. She wants to stop sitting and start jumping up and down.

Physically impossible

Every time Judy jumps up she always comes back down. She jumps off the floor into the air, but then she comes right back down to the floor every time. Now she wants it different, and that's OK with her mom. She wants to jump up and just float in the air, not touching anything. She doesn't ever want to come down.

On the way to the playground there is a really big brick wall. To get to the playground Josh has to walk way over to the side to get around this wall. Every day Josh has to walk all the way around it. Now he wants it different, and that's OK with his mom. He wants to walk right through the wall. The wall would still be there, but he would ooze right through it.

Biologically impossible

Every time Henry gets poked with a needle it really hurts. The needle pokes him and ouch, does it hurt. Now he wants to have it different, and that's OK with his mom. He wants it so that when he gets poked it *won't* hurt. He'd still get poked with the needle, but it would never hurt.

Karen is three (or four) like you. Every year she gets bigger. She keeps growing and growing. Now she wants to have it different, and that's OK with her mom. She doesn't ever want to grow again. She wants to stay the same size forever.

Source: Adapted from Schult and Wellman, forthcoming.

percent of the time). And with the biologically impossible items, the four-year-olds judged 89 percent of the time that, no, the character could not do that (the three-year-olds judged so 78 percent of the time). Obviously, even the three-year-olds appropriately judged the biologically and physically impossible acts as impossible most of the time.

Many of the children's explanations essentially, but appropriately, reiterated their judgments—for example, "It's easy; you just do it" or " You can't; it's impossible." However, at times children spontaneously went beyond these simple but acceptable explanations to mention something of the underlying forces or processes at work. These extended explanations could be coded into the categories listed previously—essentially psychological, biological, and physical explanations and a residual category of "other." In this case, both the three- and the four-year-olds produced predominantly appropriate explanations for biological as well as physical items. Specifically, 86 percent of the time that four-year-olds gave extended explanations for the physically impossible items, they gave physical explanations for them (for the three-year-olds it was 75 percent of the time); 57 percent of the time that four-year-olds gave extended explanations to the biologically impossible items, they gave biological explanations for them (for the three-year-olds it was 55 percent of the time).

Natural Language Analyses

These results concerning young children's use of psychological, physical, and biological explanations are informative yet incomplete. For example, even in the study just described, we could only ask children about a limited set of phenomena—people falling, muscles fatiguing, bodies oozing through walls. Perhaps our examples represent only a few compelling islands of clarity amid a vast sea of childhood confusion. We intentionally chose target phenomena that we hoped would be particularly clear to young children. Moreover, in testing situations such as these we directly solicited children's explanations about occurrences we made very salient. Thus it remains possible that flexible use of these distinctive explanatory reasoning systems might be limited to only special items, situations, or questions. However, if young children really do acquire several complementary explanatory theories, then that ought to be abundantly clear in a variety of everyday attempts to understand and explain their world.

To supplement our experimental investigations, we examined children's everyday explanations, captured in their conversations with their parents, siblings, and peers about ordinary events in the home (Hickling, 1996; Hickling and Wellman, 1997). These conversations provide an intriguing picture of what sort of phenomena children explain and want explained and what explanations they offer for them.

It is distinctly possible that in everyday situations very young children focus on only one type of phenomena or provide only one type of explanation. In fact, in an examination of two-year-olds' explanations, Hood and Bloom (1979) concluded that children's first causal explanations were exclusively psychological, rather than physical or biological, and exclusively about people: "The children in this study simply did not talk about causal events that occurred between physical objects in the world. . . . The children did talk about intentions and motivations" (pp. 29–30). However, by some age children must evidence a range of explanatory topics and explanations. So again we were interested in which reasoning systems children apply to which topics. That is, do they indiscriminately link various sorts of explanations to any old entity (à la Piagetian animism, realism, and artificialism), or do they strictly tie each reasoning system to proprietary objects (in an entity-based fashion)? Or, indeed, are they more appropriate than the former and more flexible than the latter?

Recently we have been examining the longitudinal transcripts of English-speaking children that are available for study through the Child Language Data Exchange System (CHILDES) (MacWhinney and Snow, 1985, 1990). This natural language database now includes systematically recorded transcripts of more than ten English-speaking children. On the basis of earlier analyses (see Bartsch and Wellman, 1995), we know that four individuals among these ten represent and provide a good view of the larger group, so we began our analyses by focusing on them. These four children—Adam, Abe, Sarah, and Ross—include one girl and three boys, two children of language researchers, one child from a professional-class family, three European Americans, and one African American. The transcripts provide extensive longitudinal language samples, collected weekly or biweekly from roughly age two to age five and including more than one hundred thousand conversations recorded at home between these young children and their parents, their siblings, and occasional visitors.

In our analyses of these transcripts we were interested in any talk centering on causes or explanations of events. We focused initially on instances in which children explicitly signaled an explanation by using identifiable causal-explanatory terms, such as *why, because, cause, how, so, if,* and *then.* Often when a child uses such terms his or her intent to express a causal explanation is especially clear, and the terms just listed include many that are used by children from an early age.

For each target utterance we considered several dimensions: syntactic form, pragmatic function, temporal reference, and so on. We focus here, however, on one conceptual distinction that we consider pivotal, the distinction between the "explained topic" versus the "explanation mode." The explanation topic identifies the phenomena to be explained, the *explanandum.* The reasoning used to explain that topic is offered in the explanation mode—the *explanans.* In the utterance "The balloon will pop because you stand on it," the topic is the balloon's popping, and the mode is someone's standing on it. Here the topic comes first, followed by the explanation for the topic, or the mode. In other sentences that order can be reversed, as in "The animals didn't like the zoo, so they went home." Here the topic is the animals' going home, and the explanation cites their not liking the zoo.

Both conversation topics and explanation modes come in different varieties; Exhibit 1.3 shows the categories we have identified. These categories are based in part on ideas we had in advance, such as the expectation that children might talk about such topics as people versus physical objects and might offer reasons that are distinctly physical rather than biological. The categories also partly emerged from children's conversations as we scrutinized their explained topics and explanation modes. For example, we distinguished talk about foods as a separate category of explained topics after we became acquainted with children's talk about food and the impossibility of deciding whether it mostly concerned *people's* eating, foods as *animal or plant* products, both, or neither. Explanation topics were identified primarily in terms of the type of object involved. Often these objects underwent some sort of motion, action, or other occurrence. (The example for persons in Exhibit 1.3 involves playing, the example for animals involves biting, and the example for physical objects involves wiggling.) As we noted in describing our experimental studies, however, motions can crosscut many entities and types; thus we concen-

Exhibit 1.3. Categories for Topics and Modes in Children's Explanations

Explanation Topics

person: "*We* have to play on the bars because I want to show you some tricks." (age 2 years, 9 months)

animal: "*The snake* bit me because he's naughty." (age 2 years, 7 months)

physical object: "*The bench* wiggles because these are loose." (age 2 years, 11 months)

plant

natural object

food

event/state

Explanation Modes

psychological (internal states, dispositions): "I'm going to get the door *because I want to*." (age 2 years, 7 months)

physical (mechanical force, changes of material state): "It [a nail] broke *because it got bent*." (age 3 years, 1 month)

biological (physiological or biochemical states, processes, mechanisms): "Good that . . . I didn't cough in Mommy's face *cause then she might get the germs*." (age 4 years, 8 months)

social/conventional (social rules, prescriptions, cultural practices or conventions): "I got this candy *because it's a prize*." (age 2 years, 11 months)

behavioral: "My hands are dirty *because I ate blueberries*." (age 2 years, 9 months)

trated on identifying the object types involved (for example, persons, animals, and physical objects).

Explanation modes, or *explanans,* come in many forms too. Our subcategories here were attempts to capture a general level of description rather than detailed explanatory arguments. Thus we coded for psychological explanations generally (which included appeals to desires, to beliefs, or to emotional states, specifically) and also for physical explanations generally (which included mentions of gravity, physical contact, or bending, specifically). We termed these categories *explanation modes* to denote this more general level of categorization. Besides the psychological, physical, and biological explanation modes, children also use social-conventional explanations, magical-fantastical explanations, and so on. In addition, we carefully identified a category of what we termed *behavioral explanations*. As in the last item on Exhibit 1.3, most of these utterances explained an overt action or activity (hands getting dirty) in terms of another action or behavior (eating blueberries). Utterances representing this explanation mode (for example, "eating blueberries") did not clearly refer to one domain (such as, say, biological aspects of eating) or another (such as physical contact from hands to berries), or they may have referred to a sort of "logic of action" at the behavioral but not clearly at the psychological level. To be conservative, we simply classified all such instances as behavioral.

The example utterances in Exhibit 1.3 are exact instances of children's speech. Each represents a type of utterance we have termed an *explanation offer,* meaning a causal statement providing an explanation in terms of both topic and mode. Explanation offers are crucial because they provide the most complete and direct opportunity to explore the relationships among children's conversational subject matter and their domains of reasoning. Other causal expressions, like *explanation requests,* by which children seek explanations, often give only a topic and so are less informative. Almost 2,500 explanation offers were provided by the four children. They also made almost 1,500 explanation requests, and they used the target causal-explanatory connectives in about 1,000 other utterances that we called *simple uses* (such as "Why?" or "Just because").

Explanation offers, explanation requests, and simple uses were provided by children at all ages, even in the earliest transcripts. Explanation offers—the more complete utterances in which children include both a topic and a mode—increased with age relative to explanation requests and simple uses. Consider children's explanations at three rough, successive age periods: two years (beginning at the first data collections, which ranged from two years and three months until two years and eleven months), three years (ranging from exactly three years to three years and eleven months) and 4 years (covering the entire fourth year). Explanation offers increased from about one-third of the

Figure 1.2. Explanation Topics, by Age Group

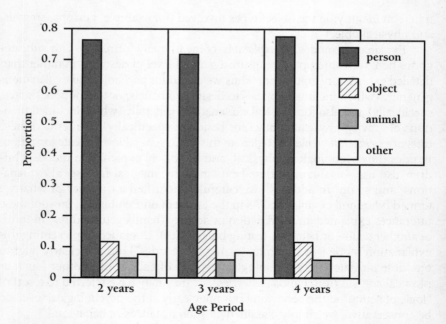

Source: Adapted from Hickling and Wellman, 1997.

utterances using the target terms at two years to more than 60 percent of them at four years. But more important than this increase is the fact that many explanation offers appeared even in the earliest period, when the children were barely two years old. Individually, each of the four children had frequent explanation offers as two-year-olds.

Both explanation offers and explanation requests allow us to address the question of what children think is worth explaining—the *topics* of their explanations and requests for explanation. From Figure 1.2 it is clear that children take great interest in people as topics for conversation and explanation. However, they also explain or request explanations for a variety of other topics, especially the nature and movements of physical objects and animals. This is true even in the earliest age period. Animals and objects thus account for more than 25 percent of all explanation offers and requests at all ages. Explanation of all other sorts of topics—plants, food, events such as thunderstorms, and so on—are relatively infrequent and so are collapsed together as "other" in Figure 1.2.

Of equal interest is what sorts of reasoning—explanation modes—the children recruited to try to explain things. As shown in Figure 1.3, children used a variety of causal explanations from early on. The sizable number of

Figure 1.3. Explanation Modes, by Age Group

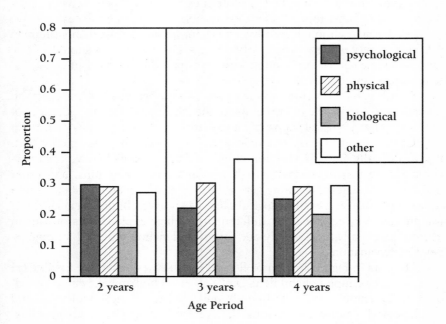

Source: Adapted from Hickling and Wellman, 1997.

"other" modes in that figure are composed mostly of social-conventional explanations, as well as the residual category of behavioral explanations outlined earlier. However, taken together, psychological plus physical plus biological explanation modes account for about 70 percent of children's explanations, suggesting that these are indeed core modes of explanation for young children.

These initial analyses make it clear that these young children comment on a variety of topics and use several sorts of reasoning, and they do so from the start of our data, early in the third year of life. But how do children fit together topics and modes, entities and reasoning systems? Here is where a focused consideration of explanation of human movements and actions again becomes important. Fortunately, of the almost 2,500 explanation offers provided by the four children, nearly 1,000 distinct instances focused on persons.

To reiterate, for adults at least, human behavior can be explained in terms of physical forces or physiological states, in addition to psychological causes. Thus if children only applied psychological explanation to persons in these conversations, that would provide evidence for the entity-based view, which claims that each explanatory reasoning system at first has its own proprietary objects. Suppose, however, that we find that children use several explanatory modes to account for human movements and acts. That could be due either to an appropriate and flexible multimodal understanding of persons or to a profound confusion about which sorts of reasoning applies to which sorts of phenomena—something along the lines of Piagetian animism, realism, and artificialism. Thus it is important to contrast explanation of persons with explanation of some other topic. Persons versus objects is an especially informative contrast, because although for adults it is appropriate to reason about human acts via a variety of these explanatory systems, physical objects should receive essentially one sort of explanation—an explanation in terms of physical systems, forces, and events.

Figure 1.4 shows children's reasoning about persons versus objects in these conversations. The figure combines the data for all three age periods, but the same pattern is readily apparent at two, three, and four years as well. What is clear from Figure 1.4 is that explanations of persons and objects differ radically. Naturally enough, children often construe people's behaviors in psychological terms—in terms of their beliefs, desires, emotions, and other psychological states. But, more generally, they also explain human action in terms of physical and even biological causes. However, children's explanations for physical objects are quite different from their explanations of human actions. Essentially there is only one sort of explanation provided for objects: *physical* explanations.

The data in Figure 1.4 can be fleshed out in two ways. First, Exhibit 1.4 gives several examples of children's explanations of human behavior. As is evident in that exhibit, these children not only applied physical, biological, and psychological reasoning to persons, they generally did so in sensible yet flexible ways. Children's exact explanations may be only vague or even incorrect (for example, "people are seeds"), but they are sensible—they sensibly apply

Figure 1.4. Explanations of Human Versus Object Behavior

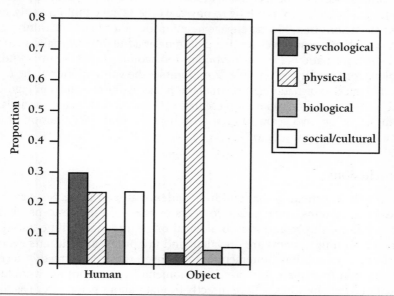

Source: Adapted from Hickling and Wellman, 1997.

Exhibit 1.4. Explanations of Human Acts

Psychological

"I talking very quiet because I don't want somebody to wake up." (Adam, age 3 years, 4 months)

"He never eats spinach cause he don't like the taste." (Ross, age 3 years, 2 months)

Biological

"He'll eat his food, because to be alive." (Ross, age 4 years, 8 months)

"I got medicine because it makes my fever go away." (Abe, age 2 years, 11 months)

"I will [be a tiny seed] because people are seeds then they grow big and then they get old." (Abe, age 3 years, 2 months)

Physical

"I pushed it because I got knocked down." (Adam, age 3 years, 3 months)

"He got a bad tooth because he fell off his bike on his face." (Ross, age 4 years, 3 months)

"The black toe hurts because Marky dropped a pan on it." (Ross, age 3 years, 8 months) physical and biological explanations to only some aspects of human activities, not others. Second, the fact that in Figure 1.4 the children *ever* applied psychological or biological thinking to physical objects, albeit infrequently, might raise suspicions that they do engage in animistic or artificialistic thinking. We certainly do not want to claim that children (or adults) never make such mistakes or speculations (see also Woolley, forthcoming). But, again, children's explanations are largely sensible. For example, the vast majority of the uses of psychological explanation to reason about physical objects tallied in Figure 1.4 involved conversations about representational objects such as toys or dolls. For example, at age two years and ten months, Ross said, "My Snoopy [doll] is growling 'cause he wants to."

Conclusions

We conclude primarily that children evidence at least three basic everyday reasoning systems as early as two years of age—physical and psychological reasoning surely, and even biological reasoning in a rudimentary form. These reasoning systems are prevalent and important in children's everyday lives and conversational interactions. Moreover, they can be readily accessed by children to explain contrived phenomena in the laboratory, including situations they may never have directly thought about before, such as bodies potentially oozing through walls. We think that even young children, two- and three-year-olds, both differentiate and coordinate these three reasoning systems in several appropriately flexible ways. By the time they are two years old, children are neither rigidly entity-based in their explanations (restricting each reasoning system to only some special, proprietary entities) nor widely confused or fantastical (applying all sorts of explanations to all sorts of indiscriminate objects). Either or both of these patterns may characterize still earlier periods of development, but at the least our findings show that children overcome such difficulties and limitations by a very young age. Young children's frequent and largely sensible explanations in our data add support to recent claims that rather than being a culminating achievement of later cognitive development, a concern with causes and explanations may be a very early contributor to cognitive development (for example, see Gelman and Kalish, 1993; Keil, 1992; Wellman and Gelman, 1992).

Our results also reveal intriguing aspects of children's naive theories of psychology, physics, and biology. For example, burgeoning research on "theory of mind" has shown that children readily apply belief- and desire-based psychological reasoning to explain voluntary human actions. This has been taken to mean that children engage in relatively appropriate psychological reasoning by at least age three or four. However, this research has not investigated an important potential error in such psychological reasoning—possible over-application of it to any and all sorts of human movements and acts. Our data show that young children not only apply psychological reasoning to human affairs but also limit this sort of reasoning appropriately, frequently distinguishing psychologically caused human acts from physically caused and biologically caused human movements.

Physical explanations also appear quite early in children's development, as might have been expected from contemporary studies revealing that even infants understand various physical principles as applied to the movements and states of physical objects (for example, see Baillargeon, Kotovsky, and Needham, 1995; Spelke, 1994). However, our findings do contrast with earlier claims that very young children's first verbal explanations focus only on psychological causes and explanations (for example, Hood and Bloom, 1979; Piaget, 1928). Moreover, even if infants implicitly recognize various physical principles as constraining physical objects, in order to provide the sorts of explanations we have documented, young children must also convert such recognition into explicit understandings and both articulate their physical reasoning in appropriate language and differentiate it from other potential explanations that use the same language (such as psychological explanations). At the very least, therefore, our data show an impressive early consolidation and articulation of infant physical causal understandings.

Our data are least complete with regard to biological understandings. There is currently great debate as to what might constitute an early but genuinely biological form of reasoning, distinctively independent from psychological or physical reasonings (for example, see Chapter Two; Atran, 1995; Carey, 1995; Wellman and Gelman, 1992). At the very least our data show that young children identify certain terms, processes, and phenomena as being outside the scope of psychological and physical reasoning—and these terms, processes, and phenomena are distinctively biological to adults. For example, consider the biological item in Exhibit 1.1. This item does not mention any biological terms; instead it mentions a psychological construct (the character's desire) and an action or movement (coming down to the ground). We know from other carefully matched items that the children in our study could and did explain this exact same action or movement in psychological and physical ways—the character "wanted to come down," or "gravity pulled her down." Yet in explaining the biological item, four-year-old children rarely offered these easily accessed psychological or physical explanations and instead spontaneously recruited such processes as fatigue and pain to explain the scenario's outcome. Overall our data suggest that at the least, young children are often reluctant to use psychological and physical reasoning to explain certain salient "biological" phenomena of everyday life.

Finally, we believe that researching young children's explanations is both easier and more revealing than is often thought. Naturally enough, perhaps, researchers examining the thinking of young children have tended to avoid eliciting explanations in favor of presenting children with simpler judgment tasks. In reaction to Piaget's classic interview studies it has been thought that articulating verbal explanations is an especially demanding task for young children and hence one that distorts rather than reveals their basic modes of thought (see Bullock, Gelman, and Baillargeon, 1982). In fact we agree with this analysis, in part; but we propose that the richness and ease of expression of children's explanations depend on the phenomena to be explained. In these three domains—everyday psychological, physical, and biological occurrences—children are early and frequently involved in using their knowledge to explain. Part of the point, the cognitive function, of these reasoning systems is to make understandable—to explain—everyday phenomena and occurrences. In *these* domains, therefore, eliciting and analyzing children's explanations proves to be an especially revealing research method. In these domains, children's knowledge is intimately tied to the task of making sense of their world, and this is essentially the task of explanation.

References

Atran, S. "Causal Constraints on Categories and Categorical Constraints on Biological Reasoning Across Cultures." In D. Sperber, D. Premack, and A. J. Premack (eds.), *Causal Cognition: A Multi-disciplinary Debate*. New York: Oxford University Press, 1995.

Backscheider, A. G., Shatz, M., and Gelman, S. A. "Preschoolers' Ability to Distinguish Living Kinds as a Function of Regrowth." *Child Development*, 1993, *64*, 1242–1257.

Baillargeon, R., Kotovsky, L., and Needham, A. "The Acquisition of Physical Knowledge in Infancy." In D. Sperber, D. Premack, and A. Premack (eds.), *Causal Cognition: A Multi-disciplinary Debate*. New York: Oxford University Press, 1995.

Bartsch, K., and Wellman, H. M. "Young Children's Attribution of Action to Beliefs and Desires." *Child Development*, 1989, *60*, 946–964.

Bartsch, K., and Wellman, H. M. *Children Talk About the Mind*. New York: Oxford University Press, 1995.

Bullock, M., Gelman, R., and Baillargeon, R. "The Development of Causal Reasoning." In W. J. Friedman (ed.), *The Developmental Psychology of Time*. Orlando: Academic Press, 1982.

Carey, S. "On the Origin of Causal Understanding." In D. Sperber, D. Premack, and A. J. Premack (eds.), *Causal Cognition: A Multi-disciplinary Debate*. New York: Oxford University Press, 1995.

Carey, S., and Spelke, E. S. "Domain-Specific Knowledge and Conceptual Change." In L. A. Hirschfeld and S. A. Gelman (eds.), *Mapping the Mind: Domain Specificity in Cognition and Culture*. Cambridge, England: Cambridge University Press, 1994.

Gelman, R., Spelke, E. S., and Meck, E. "What Preschoolers Know About Animate and Inanimate Objects." In D. Rogers and J. A. Sloboda (eds.), *The Acquisition of Symbolic Skills*. New York: Plenum, 1983.

Gelman, S. A., and Kalish, C. W. "Categories and Causality." In R. Pasnak and M. L. Howe (eds.), *Emerging Themes in Cognitive Development*. New York: Springer-Verlag, 1993.

Gelman, S. A., and Kremer, K. E. "Understanding Natural Cause: Children's Explanations of How Objects and Their Properties Originate." *Child Development*, 1991, *62*, 396–414.

Hickling, A. K. "The Emergence of Causal Explanation in Everyday Thought: Evidence from Ordinary Conversation." Unpublished doctoral dissertation, Department of Psychology, University of Michigan, 1996.

Hickling, A. K., and Wellman, H. M. "Everyday Explanation in Very Young Children." Unpublished manuscript, 1997.

Hood, L., & Bloom, L. *What, When, and How About Why: A Longitudinal Study of Early Expressions of Causality*. Monographs of the Society for Research in Child Development, no. 181. Chicago: University of Chicago Press, 1979.

Inagaki, K., and Hatano, G. "Young Children's Recognition of Commonalities Between Animals and Plants." *Child Development*, 1996, *67*, 2823–2840.

Johnson, C. N., and Wellman, H. M. "Children's Developing Conceptions of the Mind and Brain." *Child Development*, 1982, *53*, 222–234.

Keil, F. C. "The Origins of an Autonomous Biology." In M. Gunnar and M. Maratsos (eds.), *Minnesota Symposia on Child Psychology*, Vol. 25: *Modularity and Constraints in Language and Cognition*. Hillsdale, N.J.: Erlbaum, 1992.

Legerstee, M. "A Review of the Animate-Inanimate Distinction in Infancy." *Early Development and Parenting*, 1992, *1*, 59–67.

MacWhinney, B., and Snow, C. "The Child Language Data Exchange System." *Journal of Child Language*, 1985, *12*, 271–296.

MacWhinney, B., and Snow, C. "The Child Language Data Exchange System: An Update." *Journal of Child Language*, 1990, *17*, 457–472.

Piaget, J. *Judgment and Reasoning in the Child*. London: Paul Trench & Trubner, 1928.

Piaget, J. *The Child's Conception of the World*. New York: Routledge, 1929.

Rosengren, K. S., Gelman, S. A., Kalish, C. W., and McCormick, M. "As Time Goes By: Children's Early Understanding of Growth in Animals." *Child Development*, 1991, *62*, 1302–1320.

Schult, C. A., and Wellman, H. M. "Explaining Human Movements and Actions: Children's Understanding of the Limits of Psychological Explanation." *Cognition*, forthcoming.

Shultz, T. R., Wells, D., and Sardo, M. "Development of the Ability to Distinguish Intended Actions from Mistakes, Reflexes, and Passive Movements." *British Journal of Social and Clinical Psychology*, 1980, *19*, 301–310.

Smith, M. C. "Cognizing the Behavior Stream: The Recognition of Intentional Action." *Child Development*, 1978, *49*, 736–743.

Spelke, E. S. "Initial Knowledge: Six Suggestions." *Cognition*, 1994, *50*, 431–455.

Spelke, E. S., Phillips, A. T., and Woodward, A. L. "Infants' Knowledge of Object Motion and Human Action." In A. Premack (ed.), *Causal Understanding in Cognition and Culture*. Oxford, England: Clarendon Press, 1995.

Wellman, H. M., and Banerjee, M. "Mind and Emotion: Children's Understanding of the Emotional Consequences of Beliefs and Desires." *British Journal of Developmental Psychology*, 1991, *9*, 191–124.

Wellman, H. M., and Estes, D. "Early Understanding of Mental Entities: A Reexamination of Childhood Realism." *Child Development*, 1986, *57*, 910–923.

Wellman, H. M., and Gelman, S. A. "Cognitive Development: Foundational Theories of Core Domains." *Annual Review of Psychology*, 1992, *43*, 337–375.

Wellman, H. M., and Gelman, S. A. "Knowledge Acquisition in Foundational Domains." In W. Damon (ed.), *Handbook of Child Psychology* (5th ed.), Vol. 2 (D. Kuhn and R. Siegler, eds.): *Cognition, Perception and Language*. New York: Wiley, forthcoming.

Woolley, J. D. "Thinking About Fantasy: Are Children Fundamentally Different Thinkers and Believers from Adults?" *Child Development*, forthcoming.

HENRY M. WELLMAN *is professor in the Department of Psychology and research scientist at the Center for Human Growth and Development at the University of Michigan, Ann Arbor.*

ANNE K. HICKLING *is assistant professor of psychology at the University of North Carolina, Greensboro.*

CAROLYN A. SCHULT *is assistant professor of psychology at Lycoming College, Williamsport, Pennsylvania.*

Preschoolers distinguish between biological and psychological phenomena in their causal reasoning, although their biological reasoning is sometimes influenced by psychological considerations as well.

Emerging Distinctions Between Naive Biology and Naive Psychology

Kayoko Inagaki

In recent years an increasing number of developmentalists have agreed that children possess more or less coherent bodies of knowledge about important aspects of the world. They assume that such bodies of knowledge often constitute naive theories containing ontological distinctions, coherent pieces of knowledge, and causal devices or explanations as essential components (Wellman and Gelman, 1992, forthcoming). There has been consensus that naive physics and naive psychology are established very early in childhood (for example, see Carey and Spelke, 1994). In contrast, it was believed that naive biology would emerge much later, that is, in middle childhood (Carey, 1985). However, a growing number of recent studies have led leading investigators, including Carey (1995), to agree that children as young as six years of age have a form of naive biology. Thus the present hot issues are whether children under six years of age possess an autonomous domain of biological understanding, and if they do, when and how this domain emerges. The aim of this chapter is to examine the differentiations between psychology and biology in the reasoning of preschool-age children. By relying on our latest studies, I will claim that naive biology is separated from naive psychology at early ages but is sometimes influenced by psychological understandings that are established even earlier.

The research reported here was supported in part by grants in aid from the Japanese Ministry of Education to Giyoo Hatano (No. 06301015) and Kayoko Inagaki (No. 07610114). I am grateful to G. Hatano for his constructive comments on an earlier version of this chapter.

Emergence of an Autonomous Domain of Biology

I believe that rudimentary forms of both naive psychology and naive physics are established at very early ages. In contrast, I speculate that a naive biology appears later in development, during the preschool years rather than during infancy (Hatano and Inagaki, 1996). Three reasons support this speculation. Infants seldom need biological knowledge, since they do not need to take care of their health or to find food themselves. It can be argued that grasping various bodily processes, on which early understanding of biological processes rests, is more difficult than classifying observable entities in the world. Moreover, appreciating the existence of a biological domain requires the inclusion of animals and plants into an integrated category of living things, and this requires some conceptual reorganization for children.

If this speculation is correct—that is, if naive biology is added to children's knowledge systems (including naive psychology and physics) at a later stage in development—then how does the domain of biology emerge? How can we characterize children's early understanding of biological phenomena? Considering that biological entities, which include human beings, are physical entities as well and that humans are also psychological entities, three possibilities can be proposed concerning the emergence of naive biology. The first is that biology is gradually differentiated from the domain of physics. That is, to begin with biological phenomena are interpreted by children within the framework of physics. This seems unlikely, however, because recent studies have indicated that preschoolers, and sometimes even younger children, can distinguish animals from nonliving things in terms of animals' ability to make self-initiated movements (Bullock, 1985; Massey and Gelman, 1988); their manifestations of natural transformations, such as growth (Rosengren, Gelman, Kalish, and McCormick, 1991); or their distinctive internal structures (Simons and Keil, 1995). Golinkoff, Harding, Carlson, and Sexton (1984) have reported that even infants eight months of age can distinguish objects that have a capacity for self-initiated movement from those that do not. These results strongly suggest that even very young children can make the animate-inanimate distinction and thus can probably distinguish biological and psychological phenomena from physical ones.

It remains controversial, however, whether young children can distinguish plants as well as animals from nonliving things, since plants lack self-initiated movement. Atran (1994) claims that in cultures throughout the world it is common to classify all entities into four ontological categories: humans, nonhuman animals, plants, and inanimate objects, including artifacts. What is difficult for young children is to integrate both animals (including humans) and plants into a single category of living things, as opposed to nonliving things. However, recent studies indicate that preschool children differentiate both animals and plants from nonliving things in terms of living things' ability to heal by regrowth (Backscheider, Shatz, and Gelman, 1993), their natural rather than man-made origins (Gelman and Kremer, 1991), their growth and death

(Hatano and others, 1993), and their ingesting of food and water (Inagaki and Hatano, 1996). In contrast, there are few reports that young children place plants and nonliving things together in the same category. Thus the available data suggest that preschool children can distinguish living things (including animals and plants) from nonliving things. This distinction can serve as the basis for separating biology from physics at an early age.

The second possible route for the emergence of a distinct domain of biological understanding is for it to grow out of the psychological domain. Carey espouses this view. Originally (1985) she claimed that before around age ten children's predictions and explanations of biological phenomena are based on psychological reasoning. In other words, younger children neither differentiate biological phenomena from psychological ones nor recognize that biological processes (for example, those producing growth or death) are autonomous from psychological influences. Recently (1995) she lowered the age of differentiation from ten to six or seven years and moderated her claim by discarding its strong version, that young children distort all observations of biological phenomena to fit into the framework of intuitive psychology. However, she still maintains that naive biology emerges from intuitive psychology, biology's "parent" domain, and thus children younger than six do not possess a separate domain of biology.

The third possibility is that biological entities and phenomena are left unexplained or are interpreted only in terms of domain-general mechanisms until the initial naive biology is established after infancy. This position may be close to Keil's, in the sense that as soon as biological entities and phenomena begin to be construed in a domain-specific way, their interpretation is distinctly biological. Keil (1992, 1994) asserts that children aged four to seven, or even younger, engage in distinctively biological reasoning, because biology is a distinct theory or mode of construal from the beginning. He characterizes this early biology as functional or teleological: biological properties and processes are interpreted or explained in terms of what they are for. He claims that "we may be endowed with modes of construal that enable us to have extra insights into the nature of biological kinds and processes" (1992, p. 113). In other words, biological phenomena resonate strongly with the functional-teleological modes of construal, and this facilitates formation of distinctively biological reasoning from a very early age.

My position, which I elaborate and support in this chapter, is another attempt to pursue this third possibility. I agree with Keil in assuming that naive biology is a more or less privileged domain and thus emerges at an early age. However, I do not think an autonomous biology exists from the start. Rather, I believe it emerges somewhat later than physics or psychology. I also disagree with his remark, "As we look at younger and younger children, we do not see their judgments becoming more and more psychologically driven" (1992, p. 132). I think that young children's initial biological reasoning can be influenced by psychological reasoning, which is established earlier. As I describe elsewhere (Hatano and Inagaki, 1996), I assume that there are skeletal guiding principles unique to the domain of biology (namely, living things show different processes from nonliving things in that they take in vital power and grow) and that these principles lead to the construction of a distinctive theory of living things in the early years. I also assume, however, that a theory or a causal-explanatory framework for biological properties and processes has to be constructed more gradually and that its construction can be affected by prior knowledge—among other things, knowledge concerning how the mind works (that is, psychological understanding, which has been established earlier).

It is at least possible that very young children are sometimes tempted to interpret biological phenomena by borrowing from their psychological knowledge, because their biological knowledge is not mature enough to generate convincing predictions and explanations by itself. In other words, in interpreting or predicting biological phenomena, for which most adults would primarily use the most relevant biological information only, young children tend to rely on other pieces of information that may be marginally relevant, such as psychological information. In this sense, young children's understanding of biological phenomena is influenced by their psychological reasoning, as Carey (1985, 1995) indicates. However, I believe that these two naive theories are not totally undifferentiated: nutrition, growth, and reproduction play central roles in biology, whereas belief and desire do so in psychology. However, belief and desire may play marginal roles in biology, as will be shown later in the chapter.

I believe that early understandings of biology are established around the enterprise of taking in nutriments rather than that of reproduction, partly because children engage in the former but not in the latter. It is also because, thanks to the above skeletal principles, young children know that humans take vital force from food and water to maintain their vigor and that a surplus of that vital power induces their growth. Since children tend to predict or interpret the properties and behaviors of other animals and plants through person analogies (analogies using humans as the source) (Inagaki and Hatano, 1987, 1991), they would regard living things to be any entities that, like humans, acquire vital force from food and water and grow as a result of its surplus. This triangular structural relationship among food and water, active and lively states ("becomes active by taking in vital power from food"), and growth ("surplus of vital power induces growth") (Hatano and Inagaki, 1996) would be applied readily to animals. It might also be applied to plants, partly because children lack an understanding of photosynthesis. In fact, Inagaki and Hatano (1996) reported that when given brief vitalistic descriptions of human properties that apply to all living things (such as "A person becomes bigger and bigger by taking in energy from food and water"), preschool children constrained their inductive projection of these properties (for example, growth), using the category of living things. In other words, children extended given characteristics, especially growth and the taking in of food and water, to both animals and plants but not to nonliving things. This finding, coupled with Inagaki and Hatano's findings (1987, 1991) that young children apply constrained person analogies to plants to generate reasonable predictions for biological phenomena, strongly suggests that the use of personification or person analogies does not always indicate psychological reasoning, because plants are not included in the domain of psychology (Carey, 1995).

Children notice through somatosensation that several "events," uncontrolled by their intentions, are going on inside their bodies. Since children cannot see the inside of their bodies, they try to achieve "global understanding" by personifying an organ or body part (Inagaki and Hatano, 1993). The general mechanism of personification and the resultant vitalistic causality, which "fit nicely with biology" (Keil, 1992, p. 105) help children achieve the mind-body distinction and thus the clear differentiation of biology from psychology.

In what follows I describe empirical findings, from our latest studies (done in collaboration with G. Hatano) on the distinction between biology and psychology in preschool children. Specifically, I demonstrate that naive biology is a separate domain but is influenced by psychology, using phenomena that children experience in everyday life. Since I was especially interested in young (preschool-age) children in these studies, I avoided asking for lengthy explanations. Instead, I examined their predictions for biological versus psychological phenomena; that is, I examined whether they would rely on different causal devices differentially for biological and psychological phenomena.

Emergence of the Mind-Body Distinction in Children

Can young children distinguish functions of the body from those of the mind? This distinction is expected to be difficult, because biological phenomena and psychological ones are observed among a subset of animate things.

However, Inagaki and Hatano (1993) reported findings suggesting that preschool children can distinguish functions of the body from those of the mind. In this study, four-year-olds and five-year-olds were given two tasks: a modifiability task and a controllability task. In the modifiability task the children were asked whether each of three types of characteristics were modifiable and, if so, by what means. The result indicated that not only five-year-olds but also four-year-olds differentiated the three types of characteristics well in terms of their modifiability. While a great majority of the children correctly denied the modifiability of unmodifiable physical (bodily) characteristics (such as eye color), many of them answered that they could modify other physical characteristics (for example, running faster), and about half of them admitted the modifiability of mental characteristics (such as forgetfulness). A majority of the children who recognized the modifiability of the other physical characteristics asserted that modifications could be brought about by physical activities, such as exercise, diet, and so on, whereas none of them accepted physical activities as a means of modifying the mental characteristics. About half of the five-year-olds replied that to modify the mental characteristics one needed effort or determination. Some referred to mental practice (that is, concrete strategic means), as illustrated by one girl's answer: "[we can become less forgetful] if we rehearse this and that in our mind." This suggests that the children thought that mere effort or determination might play a role in modifying mental characteristics but not in modifying physical characteristics.

In the controllability task the children were asked whether organic activities within their bodies could be controlled by the children's own intentions or desires. A majority of the children in both age groups recognized that the activities of their internal organs are relatively independent of their intentions and desires.

The findings of Inagaki and Hatano (1993) are informative, but what of still younger children? As we look at younger and younger children, do their judgments become more and more psychologically driven, or not at all? Can younger children in actuality distinguish between functions of the body and those of the mind even if their judgments are apparently psychologically driven? To answer these questions, we did two experiments on the mind-body distinction.

Study 1: The Mind's Inability to Control Bodily Processes. We examined whether children aged three to five would recognize the mind's inability to control bodily processes, using a modified version of the controllability task in Inagaki and Hatano (1993). Although the 1993 study indicated that children aged four and five years recognized that internal organs' activities are beyond their control, this finding may have overestimated their ability by eliciting automatic "No" ("unable-to-do") responses, because all four items used in that study had the correct answer of "No." Thus for this study we included some filler items for which "Yes" was the expected (and correct) answer. We also examined whether children's recognition of the mind's uncontrollability is related to the development of their awareness of bodily processes.

The subjects were 20 three-year-olds, 20 four-year-olds, and 20 five-year-olds from the same kindergarten as in the 1993 study. The children were given an awareness task first and then a controllability task. The awareness task consisted of five items (feeling pain, feeling itchy, feeling full, respiration, and heartbeat), each divided into two subitems. Example questions were as follows:

1. Do you breathe? Can you show me how you breathe?
2. Have you ever felt pain? Where did you feel pain?
3. Is your heart beating, or not? Where is your heart?

The controllability task consisted of ten items—six critical items and four filler items. Three (respiration, heartbeat, and working of stomach) of the six critical items were the same as those used in 1993, except that the wording was somewhat modified on the stomach item; the other three were constructed for this study. The following questions were used:

1. Suppose Taro wants to stop breathing from morning till night. Can he do that?
2. Suppose Taro wants to stop his heartbeat. Can he do that?

3. Suppose Taro is served delicious food at a restaurant, and he becomes full. In spite of this, plenty of food remains on the table. He wants to eat all of it. Can he eat all of it if he asks his stomach to work harder to allow him to do so?

4. Suppose Taro wants to piddle when he is outside, but he cannot find a toilet nearby. Can he go without piddling until tomorrow night, if he does not want to wet his pants?

5. Suppose Taro falls down and hurts his knee. He feels pain, so he says to the pain, "Pain, Pain, go away quickly!" When he says so, can he stop feeling pain on his knee?

6. Suppose Taro gets his arm bitten by a mosquito. He feels itchy, so he says to the itch, "Itch, Itch, go away quickly!" When he says so, can he stop feeling the itch on his arm?

As discussed, filler items dealing with voluntary acts were included to prevent the children from responding "No" automatically. Two of the filler items concerned physical states and the other two biological states; both states could be controlled by means of voluntary actions. Example filler questions are as follows:

1. Suppose Taro plays in the sandbox and his hands get dirty. Can he get his hands clean again if he washes them in the water?

2. Suppose Taro gets very thirsty because he has been running. Can he slake his thirst if he drinks a glass of juice?

Items for the controllability task were given to children in random order, with the first question always being a filler item.

First we computed an awareness score for each child. We gave the respondent one point when both questions for each awareness item were answered correctly. Since the awareness task consisted of five items, the maximum score was five. The awareness scores of the three-year-olds (mean score = 1.90) were significantly lower than those of the four-year-olds (3.74) and five-year-olds (3.80), but there was no significant difference between the four- and five-year-olds' responses. This indicates that awareness of bodily processes develops markedly from age three to four. The three-year-olds had a relatively good awareness of sensations such as pain, but their awareness of the workings of internal organs, like the heart, was very poor; only 15 percent answered the heartbeat question correctly, and only 30 percent answered the question about breathing correctly. In contrast, a majority of the four- and five-year-olds were aware of their heartbeat and respiration as well as the feeling of pain and itching; 70 percent responded correctly on the heartbeat item and 85 percent on the respiration item. The awareness of feeling full was low at all age groups; percent correct was 50 percent even for five-year-olds.

Let us move on to the result of the controllability task. First, consider the children's responses to the filler items. Almost all the children in each age group correctly answered the filler questions; the mean percent correct ("Yes" response) for the four items was 86 percent for the three-year-olds and 94 percent for both the four- and the five-year-olds. This means that our subjects fully understood the questions given to them and knew about voluntary acts.

Table 2.1 shows the percentages of "unable-to-control" responses for each item of the controllability task, for each age group. For the heartbeat and respiration items, which are typical involuntary acts, both the four- and the five-year-olds significantly gave "unable-to-control" responses, while the three-year-olds showed such a tendency only insignificantly. However, the three-year-olds, as well as the four- and five-year-olds, showed a significantly larger number of "No" responses for the heartbeat and respiration items—$t(19)$ = 5.12, 9.71, 11.87, $ps < .001$, respectively—than for the two filler "biological" items (which dealt with removal of thirst by drinking juice and removal of hunger by eating food). In other words, even three-year-olds have recognized that biological or bodily phenomena such as heartbeats and respiration are less controllable than hunger or thirst, though they tend to overestimate the mind's ability to control heartbeats.

The five-year-olds clearly recognized that people cannot control the workings of their stomachs or their urinary processes simply by wanting to do so; the three- and four-year-olds' understanding of these facts was not as clear. In addition, a substantial number of the three- and four-year-olds accepted the mind's ability to control the feeling of pain and itching. Some of the children answered "Yes," with reservations, for the pain and itch questions (for example, "Yes he can [stop feeling pain], if he puts medicine or a Band-Aid on the hurt"), but most of these children changed their answer to "No" when they were asked whether the pain could be removed only by means of the subject's command, without medicine. This suggests that the children's failure on these items was in part due to the fact that they were imaging other strategies, beyond direct mental control, that could indeed mitigate pain or itching.

Study 2: The Mind's Inability to Control the Sensation and Workings of the Stomach. In Study 2 we reexamined younger children's recognition of the mind-body distinction by requiring them to distinguish direct control by

Table 2.1. Number of Subjects Who Gave "Unable-to-Control" Responses (Study 1)

Items	3 years (N = 20)	4 years (N = 20)	5 years (N = 20)
Heartbeat	11	17**	19**
Respiration	14	17**	18**
Urination	10	14	18**
Working of stomach	4*	11	17**
Feeling pain	7	12	14
Feeling itch	7	13	14

* $p < .05$; ** $p < .01$, above or below chance ($P = .5$).

the mind from indirect mental control accomplished by physical means. That is, we examined whether children would recognize distinctions between psychological and biological (or physical) means to remove pain or itching or to make a stomach work harder. We included the urination item, too (with modified wording, because the expression of the initial question was somewhat unnatural).

Additional groups of 20 three-year-olds and 20 four-year-olds from the same kindergarten were used as subjects. After they were given the awareness task, they were asked the four questions about feeling pain, feeling an itch, making the stomach work harder, and urinating, in random order. Each item included a number of subquestions depending on the children's responses. For example, the question about pain was asked as follows:

1. The child was first asked, "Suppose Masao falls down and hurts his knee. He feels pain, so he wants to stop feeling pain. Can he do that?"
2. If the answer was "Yes," the child was then asked, "How will he do that?"
3. If the answer referred to biological or physical means, such as, "put medicine on it" or "put a Band-Aid on it," Question A was asked: "If he says to the pain, 'Pain, Pain, go away quickly!' without using medicine [or putting on a Band-Aid, depending on the child's previous answer], how about the pain? Can he stop feeling pain on his knee quickly?"
4. If the child's answer to Question A was "Yes," then Question B was asked: "Suppose Taro and Jiro fall down and hurt their knees. Taro puts medicine and a Band-Aid on the hurt, while Jiro says to the pain, 'Pain, Pain, go away quickly!' without putting on medicine or a Band-Aid. Who can stop feeling pain more quickly?"
5. If the child's answer was "No" for either the initial question or Question A, he or she proceeded to the next item (itch, stomach, or urination) without further inquiry. When the child either did not answer, gave "Don't know" as the answer for the initial question, or answered "Yes" but could not tell the means, he or she was asked a question containing a hint, that is, whether Masao could stop feeling pain if he put medicine on the hurt. When the child's answer was "Yes," the two auxiliary questions then followed.

The item about feeling itchy was essentially the same as the item about feeling pain. For the stomach item, the questions were as follows:

• Question A: "If he [Masao] asks his stomach to work harder, can he eat all of it?"
• Question B: "Suppose Taro and Jiro are served delicious food at a restaurant, and they become full. In spite of this, plenty of food remains on the table. Taro tries to eat all of it after taking some exercise. Jiro tries to eat all of it by asking his stomach to work harder to allow him to do so. Who can eat all of it?"

If in response to the initial question the child gave no answer, said "Don't know," or answered "Yes" but could not tell the means, a hint was provided, as follows: "Can Masao eat all of it after taking some exercise?"

The urinating item was asked as follows: "Suppose Masao drinks a lot of juice before going to bed. He wants to piddle in the middle of night, but he hates to go to the toilet at night, so he wants to stay in bed without piddling until morning. Can he do that?" If a child's answer was "Yes" he or she was asked, "How will he do that?" Irrespective of the child's response, he or she proceeded to the next item without further inquiry.

Table 2.2 shows the children's responses for all except the urinating item. For the pain item, seven each of the three- and the four-year-olds answered "No" (unable to control) to the initial question. Almost all of the other thirteen children in each age group who answered "Yes" to the initial question referred to medicine or a Band-Aid as the means of removing the pain; in other words, none of them spontaneously gave a mental strategy for getting rid of the pain. Out of these thirteen, 5 three-year-olds denied the mind's ability to control pain in response to Question A, and 9 four-year-olds did so; thus, 12 three-year-olds and 16 four-year-olds "spontaneously" recognized that the pain could not be removed by their desire or command. Out of the children who acknowledged in response to Question A that the mind could control pain, 5 three-year-olds and 3 four-year-olds chose biological means as being more efficient than mental ones in their answer to Question B. This indicates that (when their responses to Questions A and B are taken into account) 85 percent (seventeen out of twenty) of the three-year-olds and 90 percent (nineteen out of twenty) of the four-year-olds recognized that bodily functions are beyond direct mental control; these percentages were significantly higher than chance (chance probability = .5). For the itch item, similar responses were obtained; 80 percent of the three-year-olds and 100 percent of the four-year-olds recognized the mind's inability to control itching.

For the stomach item, six of the three-year-olds and twelve of the four-year-olds answered "No" (unable to control) to the initial question. Out of the children who answered "Yes" to the initial question, only two children of age four gave any strategy for eating more, but almost all of them acknowledged that taking exercise was a good strategy for eating more, in response to the question with a hint. Two of the three-year-olds and three of the four-year-olds denied that asking the stomach to work harder was a good strategy for Question A. Even among those children who acknowledged the possibility of mental control for Question A, ten (6 three-year-olds and 4 four-year-olds) saw physical means (taking exercise) as more effective than asking the stomach to work harder when they were required to choose one option in response to Question B. This indicates that 70 percent (fourteen out of twenty) of the three-year-olds and 95 percent (nineteen out of twenty) of the four-year-olds recognized that the workings of the stomach cannot be controlled by the mind. These percentages were nearly significantly higher for the three-year-olds and significantly higher for the four-year-olds than chance (chance probability = .5).

Table 2.2. Children's Responses to Three Questions About
the Controllability Task (Study 2)

	Feeling pain		Feeling itch		Working of stomach	
	3 years	4 years	3 years	4 years	3 years	4 years
"Unable" response to the initial question	7	7	10	8	6	12
"Able" response, but denied mental means (Question A)	5	9	2	12	2	3
Spontaneous denial of mind's control-lability	(12)	(16)	(12)	(20)	(8)	(15)
"Able" response, but weighing more physical means (Question B)	5	3	4	—	6	4

Note: There were 20 three-year-olds and 20 four-year-olds.

For the urination item, nine (45 percent) of the three-year-olds and eighteen (90 percent) of the four-year-olds denied the mind's ability to control bodily processes in their response to the initial question. Furthermore, none of the children who answered "Yes" gave any strategy for controlling urination. Compared with the result of Study 1, the question used in Study 2 improved the four-year-olds' performance but not the three-year-olds'.

Finally, consider the relationship demonstrated in these studies between children's awareness of bodily processes and their recognition of the mind's inability to control them. We found significant and nearly significant correlations between the awareness score and the mind's uncontrollability score in Study 1 (.39), and Study 2 (.27). These indicate that the more the children were aware of their bodily processes, the more often they recognized that bodily processes operate independent of their intentions. In neither of the studies, however, were partial correlations significant (with the effect of age partialled out), because the awareness score was highly correlated with age.

In sum, Studies 1 and 2 strongly suggest that children as young as three years of age distinguish biological (bodily) processes from psychological ones, insofar as a majority of them recognize that bodily processes cannot be controlled simply by intentions or desires. It also seems, however, that some younger children's reasoning about biological phenomena can be influenced by psychological factors, such as intentions or desires. When asked questions in a more or less general way, the three-year-olds, and some of the four-year-olds, apparently tended to believe in the mind's ability to control some bodily processes. When asked more specific questions, however, such as questions eliciting strategies for affecting bodily processes, even the three-year-olds referred to biological (physical) strategies and not mental ones. More than half the three-year-olds and a majority of the four-year-olds who were required to choose between biological and mental means chose the former as more efficient. Awareness of internal bodily processes develops markedly around four years of age, and as it develops, children's judgments about the controllability of bodily processes may become more independent from psychological causal variables, though further study is needed to clarify this relationship.

Young Children's Understanding of Illness

If it is true that although young children differentiate bodily functions from mental ones their judgments about biological processes are sometimes influenced by psychological reasoning, then this tendency should be observed in young children's understanding of illness as well. Traditionally it has been believed that young children have great difficulty understanding causes of illness and thus are likely to accept social or psychological explanations such as immanent justice (for example, Bibace and Walsh, 1981; Kister and Patterson, 1980). However, a number of recent studies have provided evidence suggesting that even preschool children have some biological understanding of the causes of illness (for example, Siegal, 1988; Springer and Ruckel, 1992; Kalish, 1996).

These studies to date have primarily examined whether children understand the contribution of an exogenous factor (such as exposure to germs) to becoming ill. The exogenous factor is not by itself sufficient to make a person ill, although it is often a necessary condition. Whether or not a person who is exposed to such factors will get sick depends on his or her endogenous condition or bodily resistance. For example, imbalanced nutrition will erode a person's vital power and thus weaken his or her resistance to becoming ill. Knowledge about endogenous conditions is important even for young children. Thus in Study 3 we examined whether preschool children would rely on biological factors (that is, factors leading to the erosion of vital power) but not social or psychological factors as influencing bodily resistance to illness.

Study 3: Bodily Resistance to Illness. The subjects were 20 four-year-olds, 20 five-year-olds, and 20 six-year-olds from the same kindergarten as in Studies 1 and 2. The mean age of the four- and five-year-olds in this study was five months younger than that of the corresponding age groups in Studies 1 and 2, so children of age three were not included in this study.

The subjects were interviewed individually. They were presented with a pair of drawings of two boys and were told that each boy behaved differently in his everyday life in two areas: his health-related (biological) behavior (for example, one boy eats a lot every day, but the other eats little; one boy eats lots of vegetables, but the other eats few vegetables; one boy airs out his room occasionally by opening his windows, but the other does not air out his room; one boy goes to bed early, but the other stays up late watching TV) and his social or psychological behavior (one boy often lies, but the other doesn't; one boy often hits or pinches a friend, but the other is a good friend). The subjects were then asked, "When these two boys, X and Y, play with a child who has a cold and is coughing a lot, which is more likely to catch the cold, or are both equally likely?"

Results indicated that there were almost no developmental differences in judgment for the four biological items: a majority of the children in each age group indicated that the boy who ate little, did not air out his room, ate few vegetables, and stayed up late would be more likely to catch a cold than the boy who ate a lot, aired out his room, ate a lot of vegetables, and went to bed early. Even the four-year-olds were considerably correct in their judgments, with the one exception being their responses to the airing-out-the-room item.

Although the four- and five-year-olds could give few reasons for their choices, about half of the six-year-olds justified their selection of the boy who eats little and eats few vegetables as the individual more likely to catch a cold. For example, a child of age six years and three months said, "[A boy who has] little nutrition does not have energy, so germs easily enter his body." Another child said, "When this boy X eats a lot, his throat is full of nutriments. This boy Y eats little, so his throat is not full of nutriments, and so the coughing can pass through his throat." Still another child said, "A boy who eats a lot of vegetables is a vigorous child, so he is unlikely to catch cold." Although a majority of our subjects could not give reasonable explanations for why a boy who does not air out his room is more likely to catch a cold, one of the six-year-olds justified his choice by saying, "Old air makes this boy weaker, and when he plays with a child who has a cold, he will be much weaker and catch cold." Taking into account the fact that the choice patterns of the four- and five-year-olds were very similar to those of the six-year-olds, it is highly likely that the children of ages four and five, like the six-year-olds, considered that a scarcity of energy or vital power would weaken bodily resistance to illness, although they did not explicitly say this.

These children also indicated that social or psychological factors would influence a person's resistance to becoming ill. More specifically, a majority not only of the younger children but also of the six-year-olds answered that the boy who often hit or pinched a friend or told a lie was more likely to catch a cold than the boy who was a good friend and never lied. Only 12.5 percent of the five- and six-year-olds' responses either included or rejected both social factors as influential (which would indicate that telling a lie or hitting or pinching a friend was irrelevant to catching a cold). In other words, most children recognized that disease is caused by biological factors, but at the same time they believed that social or psychological factors were not totally irrelevant to becoming ill. Does this mean that, contrary to the findings on the mind's inability to control bodily processes in Studies 1 and 2, children of ages four to six years cannot differentiate biological phenomena from social (psychological) phenomena in terms of the causes of illness? To answer this question, we performed Study 4, using another group of children from the same kindergarten.

Study 4: Biological Versus Social or Psychological Factors Affecting Illness. In this study we examined, with a conflict task, whether children would differentially apply biological factors and social or psychological factors to biological and social or psychological phenomena. Specifically, we investigated whether children would regard biological factors (such as nutrition) as more important in resisting illness and social or psychological factors (such as morals) as more important to being a likable person. The conflict task, consisting of six biological items (about catching a cold) and six social or psychological items (about being invited to a party), was constructed by combining three biological states (eats a lot versus eats a little; eats a lot of vegetables versus eats few vegetables; wears a thick sweater outside in winter versus wears a thin short-sleeve shirt) and three social or psychological ones (tells a lie versus never lies; hits or pinches a friend versus is a good friend; does mischief often versus does not do mischief) in a mismatched fashion. In other words, "good" biological traits were paired with "bad" psychological or social traits— "eats a lot of vegetables and hits or pinches friends"— or vice versa.

The subjects were 20 four-year-olds and 20 five-year-olds. They were presented with a pair of drawings depicting two children (shown in Figure 2.1) and were asked which child, if any, would be more likely to catch a cold: child X (on the left in the figure), who is in good condition physically (for example, eats a balanced diet) but behaves badly (often hits and misbehaves),

Figure 2.1. An Example of the Stimulus Cards Used in Study 4

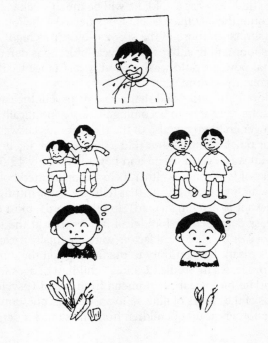

or child Y, who is in poor condition physically (is malnourished) but behaves well (is a good friend). For example, "When playing with a child who has a cold and is coughing a lot, which is more likely to catch a cold (or are both equally likely), a boy who often hits or pinches his friend but eats a lot of vegetables every day or a boy who is a good friend but eats few vegetables?" After finishing the six biological items, the children were also asked six social items—that is, which of the two children (X or Y) would be more likely to be invited to a birthday party by a classmate?

We classified the children's responses into three categories for both the biological items (that is, those pertaining to catching a cold) and the social items (those pertaining to being invited to a party):

- Biological-cue-dominant response: making a choice by relying more on the biological condition than the moral one
- Social-cue-dominant response: making a choice by relying less on the biological condition than the moral one
- Equivalent response: choosing both or neither alternatives

Statistical analyses showed significant differences in the numbers of biological-cue-dominant responses to the cold and party questions in both the four-year-olds ($t[19]$ = 3.02, p <.05) and the five-year-olds ($t[19]$ = 11.00, p <.001). This indicates that these children considered biological (for example, nutritional) factors to be more important for mediating becoming ill and social or psychological factors as critical for popularity. In other words, not only the five-year-olds but also the four-year-olds clearly differentiated biological phenomena from social or psychological phenomena.

Figure 2.2 shows the percentages of the three types of responses for the biological (cold) items and the social-psychological (party) items. The five-year-olds made biological-cue-dominant responses more often than social-cue-dominant responses for the biological phenomena, and they made social-cue-dominant responses more often than biological-cue-dominant responses for the social-psychological phenomena. They justified their choices by referring to biological factors for the cold questions and to moral (or behavioral) factors for the party questions. In contrast, the four-year-olds showed almost as many social-cue-dominant responses as biological-cue-dominant responses for the cold question, although they made social-cue-dominant responses more often for the party questions. This suggests that the four-year-olds' reasoning for biological phenomena was more influenced by psychological considerations than was the five-year-olds' biological reasoning.

Conclusions

From the studies described in this chapter we can conclude that by age four, at least, children distinguish biological phenomena from psychological ones in their reasoning, although their reasoning about biological phenomena is

Figure 2.2. Percentage of Responses for the Biological (Cold) and Social-Psychological (Party) Items

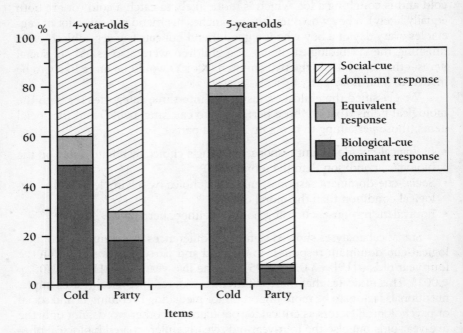

sometimes influenced by social or psychological variables, especially when these variables are salient or biological causal factors are not explicitly referred to. Even three-year-olds recognize that internal bodily functions such as heartbeat and respiration are less controllable than hunger or thirst, even though they tend to overestimate the mind's ability to control the former functions. They rely on biological (physical) strategies and not mental ones to affect bodily processes (to remove pains and itches, for instance). At age four children choose biological (for example, nutritional) factors as more important for mediating disease transmission and social or psychological factors as critical for popularity.

Of course, there remains a possibility that a rudimentary form of naive biology exists apart from the other domains (naive psychology and physics) at an even earlier age, as suggested by Wellman, Hickling, and Schult in Chapter One. The point at which an autonomous domain of biology is established will differ depending on the criteria used to define that domain. If we consider an understanding of living things (including plants) and bodily processes as critical for the establishment of biological reasoning, then it seems likely that a domain of biology emerges during the preschool years. However, if we take understandings of a very limited range of biological phenomena, such as animals' bodily construction and life-sustaining behaviors, as indices of the existence of an autonomous domain of naive biology, then such a domain may exist even in infancy or toddlerhood. Anyway, it will be rewarding to further investigate how infants and toddlers "interpret" biological phenomena because it will contribute to our understandings of the origin and characterization of an autonomous domain of biology.

As described above, young children's reasoning about biological phenomena is sometimes affected by psychological causal factors, for a number of different reasons. Children may borrow some knowledge from psychology in predicting or interpreting biological phenomena because they lack usable biological knowledge. They may take psychological factors into consideration because, although a biological knowledge system exists for them, their psychological knowledge system, established earlier, is more salient in their minds. Another possibility is that they rely on psychology because they do not know when to use biological knowledge. As indicated by Gutheil, Vera, and Keil (forthcoming), who did inductive projection studies with preschoolers, young children have access to multiple belief systems for understanding living things, and the psychological system may be the default option among them. Still another possibility is that young children's minds may reflect the basic fact that the mind and body are interdependent, not independent, a view reflected in Eastern approaches to health and illness. In light of this possibility, it will be particularly intriguing to study the interrelationships between the domains of naive biology and psychology from developmental and cross-cultural perspectives.

References

Atran, S. "Core Domains Versus Scientific Theories: Evidence from Systematics and Itza-Maya Folkbiology." In L. A. Hirschfeld and S. A. Gelman (eds.), *Mapping the Mind: Domain Specificity in Cognition and Culture.* Cambridge, England: Cambridge University Press, 1994.

Backscheider, A. G., Shatz, M., and Gelman, S. A. "Preschoolers' Ability to Distinguish Living Kinds as a Function of Regrowth." *Child Development,* 1993, *64,* 1242–1257.

Bibace, R., and Walsh, M. E. "Children's Conceptions of Illness." In R. Bibace and M. E. Walsh (eds.), *Children's Conceptions of Health, Illness, and Bodily Functions.* New Directions for Child Development, no. 14. San Francisco: Jossey-Bass, 1981.

Bullock, M. "Animism in Childhood Thinking: A New Look at an Old Question." *Developmental Psychology,* 1985, *21,* 217–225.

Carey, S. *Conceptual Change in Childhood.* Cambridge, Mass.: MIT Press, 1985.

Carey, S. "On the Origin of Causal Understanding." In D. Sperber, D. Premack, and A. J. Premack (eds.), *Causal Cognition: A Multi-disciplinary Debate.* New York: Oxford University Press, 1995.

Carey, S., and Spelke, E. S. "Domain-Specific Knowledge and Conceptual Change." In L. A. Hirschfeld and S. A. Gelman (eds.), *Mapping the Mind: Domain Specificity in Cognition and Culture.* Cambridge, England: Cambridge University Press, 1994.

Gelman, S. A., and Kremer, K. E. "Understanding Natural Cause: Children's Explanations of How Objects and Their Properties Originate." *Child Development,* 1991, *62,* 396–414.

Golinkoff, R. M., Harding, C. G., Carlson, V., and Sexton, M. E. "The Infant's Perception of Causal Events: The Distinction Between Animate and Inanimate Objects." In L. P. Lipsitt and C. Rovee-Collier (eds.), *Advances in Infancy Research.* Norwood, N.J.: Ablex, 1984.

Gutheil, G., Vera, A., and Keil, F. C. "All Animals Are Equal, but Some Are More Equal Than Others: The Relations Between Patterns of Induction and Biological Beliefs in Development." *Cognition*, forthcoming.

Hatano, G., and Inagaki, K. "Cognitive and Cultural Factors in the Acquisition of Intuitive Biology." In D. R. Olson and N. Torrance (eds.), *Handbook of Education and Human Development: New Models of Learning, Teaching and Schooling*. Cambridge, Mass.: Blackwell, 1996.

Hatano, G., and others. "The Development of Biological Knowledge: A Multi-national Study." *Cognitive Development*, 1993, *8*, 47–62.

Inagaki, K., and Hatano, G. "Young Children's Spontaneous Personification as Analogy." *Child Development*, 1987, *58*, 1013–1020.

Inagaki, K., and Hatano, G. "Constrained Person Analogy in Young Children's Biological Inference." *Cognitive Development*, 1991, *6*, 219–231.

Inagaki, K., and Hatano, G. "Young Children's Understanding of the Mind-Body Distinction." *Child Development*, 1993, *64*, 1534–1549.

Inagaki, K., and Hatano, G. "Young Children's Recognition of Commonalities Between Animals and Plants." *Child Development*, 1996, *67*, 2823–2840.

Kalish, C. W. "Preschoolers' Understanding of Germs as Invisible Mechanisms." *Cognitive Development*, 1996, *11*, 83–106.

Keil, F. C. "The Origins of an Autonomous Biology." In M. Gunnar and M. Maratsos (eds.), *Minnesota Symposia on Child Psychology*, Vol. 25: *Modularity and Constraints in Language and Cognition*. Hillsdale, N.J.: Erlbaum, 1992.

Keil, F. C. "The Birth and Nurturance of Concepts by Domain: The Origins of Concepts of Living Things." In L. A. Hirschfeld and S. A. Gelman (eds.), *Mapping the Mind: Domain Specificity in Cognition and Culture*. Cambridge, England: Cambridge University Press, 1994.

Kister, M. C., and Patterson, C. J. "Children's Conceptions of the Causes of Illness: Understanding of Contagion and Use of Immanent Justice." *Child Development*, 1980, *51*, 839–846.

Massey, C. M., and Gelman, R. "Preschoolers' Ability to Decide Whether a Photographed Unfamiliar Object Can Move Itself." *Developmental Psychology*, 1988, *24*, 307–317.

Rosengren, K. S., Gelman, S. A., Kalish, C. W., and McCormick, M. "As Time Goes By: Children's Early Understanding of Growth in Animals." *Child Development*, 1991, *62*, 1302–1320.

Siegal, M. "Children's Knowledge of Contagion and Contamination as Causes of Illness." *Child Development*, 1988, *59*, 1353–1359.

Simons, D. J., and Keil, F. C. "An Abstract to Concrete Shift in the Development of Biological Thought: The *Insides* Story." *Cognition*, 1995, *56*, 129–163.

Springer, K., and Ruckel, J. "Early Beliefs About the Cause of Illness: Evidence Against Immanent Justice." *Cognitive Development*, 1992, *7*, 429–443.

Wellman, H. M., and Gelman, S. A. "Cognitive Development: Foundational Theories of Core Domains." *Annual Review of Psychology*, 1992, *43*, 337–375.

Wellman, H. M., and Gelman, S. A. "Knowledge Acquisition in Foundational Domains." In W. Damon (ed.), *Handbook of Child Psychology* (5th ed.), Vol. 2 (D. Kuhn and R. Siegler, eds.): *Cognition, Perception and Language*. New York: Wiley, forthcoming.

KAYOKO INAGAKI is professor of education at Chiba University, Japan.

Clinical case studies, family studies, and experimental evidence show that children with autism show both deficits in folk psychology and superiorities in folk physics.

Are Children with Autism Superior at Folk Physics?

Simon Baron-Cohen

Just over ten years ago my colleagues and I asked the question "Do children with autism have a 'theory of mind'?" (Baron-Cohen, Leslie, and Frith, 1985). Using a false-belief test (Wimmer and Perner, 1983) we arrived at a preliminary answer. The majority of children with autism failed the test, which suggested that they were indeed impaired in the development of a theory of mind.

A theory of mind, also called a *folk psychology,* is the main way in which human beings are believed to make sense of actions (Carey, 1985; Dennett, 1978; Heider and Simmel, 1944). That is, attributing mental states (such as beliefs, desires, and intentions) and knowledge to actors seems to be the automatic way in which we compute the causes of actions and predict future ones. John Morton and his colleagues (Morton, Frith, and Leslie, 1991) coined an incisive, succinct term for this process: *mentalizing.*

In the ten years since this first test of mentalizing in children with autism there have been more than thirty further experimental tests of the hypothesis, the vast majority revealing profound impairments in the development of folk psychological understanding in autistic individuals. These tests are reviewed elsewhere (Baron-Cohen, 1995; Baron-Cohen, Tager-Flusberg, and Cohen, 1993). This impairment includes deficits in understanding that seeing leads to knowing (Baron-Cohen and Goodhart, 1994), distinguishing mental from physical entities (Baron-Cohen, 1989a), and making appropriate distinctions

---

The author was supported by the Medical Research Council, the Wellcome Trust, and the Gatsby Foundation in preparing this chapter. The editors provided much appreciated feedback on the first draft of the chapter.

between appearance and reality (Baron-Cohen, 1989a). This deficit in autistic children's folk psychology is thought to underlie the difficulties they have in social and communicative development (Baron-Cohen, 1988) and the development of imagination (Baron-Cohen, 1987).

Beyond Folk Psychology

So far we know something about the development of a folk psychology in autism. But there is more to cognition than folk psychology. In this section I introduce the notion of a *folk physics*.

Consider Brentano's thesis ([1874] 1970) that in this universe there are only two kinds of entities: those that have intentionality and those that do not. This roughly corresponds to the distinction between animate and inanimate objects, in that inanimate things (like rocks and tables) appear to have no intentionality, but most animate things (like mice and men) are treated as if they do. Intentionality is defined as the capacity to refer or point to things other than oneself. A rock cannot point to anything. It just is. In contrast, a mouse can *look at* a piece of cheese, it can *want* the piece of cheese, and so on. The animate-inanimate distinction does not quite cover the intentional-nonintentional distinction, in that plants are of course animate (they are alive), so the distinction is probably better covered by the concept of agency (Premack, 1990). Agents have intentionality, and nonagents do not.

The task for us as information processors is to compute the causes for the actions of these two classes of entities. Dennett's claim (1978) is that humans, from birth to the grave, use folk psychology to deduce the cause of agents' actions and folk physics to deduce the cause of the actions (that is, movement) of any other entity. Why does a rock roll down a hill? If an agent is involved, then the event is interpreted as being caused by an intention (the agent's intention to throw the rock, to roll it, to kick it, and so on). If no agent is involved, then the event is interpreted in terms of a physical causal force (the rock rolls because it is hit by another object, because of gravity, and so on).

Sperber, Premack, and Premack (1995) suggest that humans alone have the reflective capacity to be concerned about causality and that "causal cognition" falls broadly into the two domains of folk psychology and folk physics. (These are the two "big" cognitive domains, but of course others do exist, such as folk biology and folk mathematics. It remains to be seen if or when in development folk mathematics or biology are independent of folk physics rather than being a subset of it. In this chapter I confine myself to folk psychology versus folk physics.) Folk psychology (explanations of the mental or intentional causes behind agent-initiated events) appears to be present from at least twelve months of age (Baron-Cohen, 1994; Gergely, Nadasdy, Gergely, and Biro, 1995; Premack, 1990). Folk physics (explanations of the physical causes of any other kind of event) is present even earlier in human ontogeny (Baillargeon, Kotovsky, and Needham, 1995; Leslie and Keeble, 1987; Spelke, Phillips, and Woodward, 1995).

Leslie (1995) captures this distinction by proposing that two independent modules are part of the infant's cognitive architecture: a theory of mind mechanism (ToMM) and a theory of bodies mechanism (ToBy). Baron-Cohen (1994) suggests that although a full-blown theory of mind may take several years to develop, a more restricted intentionality detector (ID), along the lines proposed by Premack (1990), does appear to be part of our causal cognition in infancy.

Let us return to considering autism. Clearly a crucial contrast case in terms of understanding cognition in autism would be to look at the folk physics of autistic individuals. We know that in autism there is an impairment in folk psychology. How circumscribed is this cognitive impairment in autistics? Does it leave their folk physics intact? Or might their folk physics be superdeveloped (either in compensation for their underdeveloped folk psychology or for other, possibly genetic, reasons)?

Autism and Folk Physics

If children with autism have an impaired folk physics, this might suggest that the cause of their problems in discerning intentionality is a problem with "theory building" per se (Carey, 1985). However, there are reasons to suspect that not only is their folk physics intact, it may even be superior to that of normally developing children.

Two classes of evidence can be brought to bear on this claim of superior folk physics in autistic children: clinical anecdotes and experimental results. Regarding the former, there is no shortage of clinical descriptions of autistic children who are fascinated by machines (the paragon of nonintentional systems). One of the earliest clinical accounts was by Bettelheim (Bettelheim, 1968), who describes the case of "Joey, the mechanical boy." This child with autism was obsessed with drawing pictures of machines (both real and fictitious) and with explaining his own behavior and that of others in purely mechanical terms. Bettelheim injected his psychoanalytic point of view into his interpretation of these drawings, but we can leave such interpretations to one side. The bare facts are that the boy was obsessed with machines. On the face of it, this would suggest that he had a well-developed folk physics.

The clinical literature reveals hundreds of cases of children obsessed by machines. Parents' accounts (Hart, 1989; Lovell, 1978; Park, 1967) are a rich source of such descriptions. Indeed, it is hard to find a clinical account of autism in children that does *not* involve the child's being obsessed by some machine or another. Typical examples include extreme fascination with electrical towers, burglar alarms, vacuum cleaners, washing machines, video players, trains, planes, and clocks. Sometimes the "machine" that is the object of the child's obsession is quite simple (a system of drain pipes, the designs of windows, and so on).

Of course, being fascinated by a machine does not necessarily imply understanding it, but in fact most of these anecdotes reveal that children with autism also have a precocious understanding of machines. Autistic children (at least, those with enough language) have been described as holding forth, like "little professors," on their favorite subject or area of expertise, often failing to detect that their listener has long since become bored by the subject. The apparently precocious mechanical understanding of such children suggests that their folk physics might be outstripping their folk psychology in development.

The anecdotal evidence includes not just an obsession with machines but also an obsession with other kinds of physical systems. Examples include obsessions with the weather (meteorology), the formation of mountains (geography), the motion of the planets (astronomy), and the classification of lizards (taxonomy). That is, the folk physics of autistic children embraces both artifactual and natural kinds. In this chapter I use the term *folk physics* both in a narrow way, to refer to people's understanding of physical causality, and in a broader way, to encompass all nonintentional aspects of the physical world, whether causal or not.

Figure 3.1. Example of a Physical-Causal Story Sequence

Source: Based on Baron-Cohen, Leslie, and Frith, 1986.

Figure 3.2. Example of an Intentional-Causal Story Sequence

Source: Based on Baron-Cohen, Leslie, and Frith, 1986.

Experimental Evidence

Experimental studies have revealed evidence leading toward the same conclusion as the anecdotal clinical evidence just described, that children with autism not only have an intact folk physics but also in fact demonstrate accelerated or superior development in this domain (relative to their folk psychology). First, using a picture-sequencing method we found that children with autism performed significantly better than mental age–matched controls in sequencing stories involving physical causation (Baron-Cohen, Leslie, and Frith, 1986). The children with autism also described more physical causes in their verbal accounts of the picture sequences, compared to intentional causes. An example of a physical explanation, or cause, in a story sequence is shown in Figure 3.1 (tripping and falling), and an example of a contrasting intentional cause in a story sequence is shown in Figure 3.2 (a false belief causing surprise).

Second, two studies (Leekam and Perner, 1991; Leslie and Thaiss, 1992) found that children with autism showed good understanding of a camera. In these studies a child was shown a scene in which an object was located in one position (A). The child was encouraged to take a photo of this scene, using a Polaroid camera. While the experimenter and the child were waiting for the photo to develop, the scene was changed: the object was moved to a new position (B). The experimenter then turned to the child and asked where in the photo the object would be, position A or B? These studies found that children with autism could accurately infer what would be depicted in the photograph even though the photograph was at odds with the current visual scene. This contrasted with their poor performance on a false-belief test.

What was particularly important about these experiments was that the structure of the "false-photo task" exactly paralleled the structure of the false-belief task. The key difference is that in the (folk psychology–based) false-belief test a *person* sees the scene, and then the object is moved from A to B while that person is absent. Hence the person holds a belief that is at odds with the current visual scene. In the false-photo task a *camera* records the scene, and then the object is moved from A to B while the camera is not in use. Hence the camera contains a picture that is at odds with the current visual scene. The pattern of the autistic children's results on these two tests was interpreted to demonstrate that although their understanding of mental representations was impaired, their understanding of physical representations was not. Similar patterns have been found on tests of drawings and models (Charman and Baron-Cohen, 1992, 1995). But the false-photo test is also evidence that the mechanical understanding of individuals with autism (their folk physics) outstrips their folk psychology.

Let us now turn to a third piece of evidence. In a study examining children's understanding of the functions of the brain, significantly more children with autism than mental age–matched controls mentioned the brain's functional (physiological) role in producing action (Baron-Cohen, 1989a). In contrast, in the same study children with autism were significantly less likely to mention mentalistic functions of the brain or mind. Once again the same pattern of superior folk physics and inferior folk psychology among autistic children is seen. Our concept of the brain involves physical-causal events, while our concept of the mind involves intentional-causal events.

Fourth, in a study of the animate-inanimate distinction in autism (Baron-Cohen, 1989a) it was found that school-age children with autism were perfectly able to distinguish two different kinds of moving objects: mechanical versus animate. (Mechanical objects were things like vacuum cleaners and cars. Animate objects were things like mice and men.) This is additional evidence that their folk physics is intact.

Fifth, there is evidence that children with autism show no delays in reaching object permanence (they solve the A-not-B search problem at the normal point in development) (Sigman, Ungerer, Mundy, and Sherman, 1987). This latter finding also shows that their understanding of physical objects is normal. It is, incidentally, inconsistent with a general-executive-dysfunction account of autism (Russell, 1996), which would predict perseveration at location A.

Sixth, high-functioning adults with autism or Asperger Syndrome (AS)—an alternative diagnosis thought to characterize a subgroup of high-functioning autistics—all selected to be of normal intelligence, are *faster* on the Embedded Figures Test than matched controls (Jolliffe and Baron-Cohen, forthcoming). In contrast, such able subjects show persisting impairments on an adult-level test of folk psychology (Baron-Cohen, Jolliffe, Mortimore, and Robertson, forthcoming). This replicates and extends a similar finding using the Embedded Figures Test with children with autism (Shah and Frith, 1983). Although this does not index their physical-causal cognition, it again shows that aspects of their folk physics (spatial abilities) are actually superior to those of normal people and certainly outstrip their own folk psychology. (In this example the concept of folk physics is used more broadly to refer to understanding of the physical world, whether causal or otherwise.)

Evidence from Family Studies

Family studies add to this picture. Parents of children with AS also show mild but significant deficits on an adult mentalizing task, mirroring the deficit in folk psychology seen in patients with autism or AS (Baron-Cohen and Hammer, "Parents of Children with Asperger Syndrome," forthcoming). According to the current argument, since autism and AS appear to have a strong heritable component (Bailey and others, 1995; Bolton and others, 1994; Folstein and Rutter, 1977; Le Couteur and others, 1996), one should expect that parents of children with autism or AS should be overrepresented among occupations in which possessing superior folk physics would be an advantage but having a deficit in folk psychology would not necessarily be a disadvantage. The paradigm occupation for such a cognitive profile is engineering.

A recent study of one thousand families found that fathers and grandfathers (patrilineal and matrilineal) of children with autism or AS were more than twice as likely to work in the field of engineering, compared to control groups (Baron-Cohen and others, forthcoming). Table 3.1 summarizes these results. Indeed, 28.4 percent of children with autism or AS had at least one relative (father or grandfather) who was an engineer. (This percentage cannot be derived directly from Table 3.1, because in some families there was more than one relative who was an engineer.)

This raises the possibility that the cognitive phenotype of the parents (one or both of whom carry the genes for autism or AS) involves a superiority in folk physics alongside a relative deficit in folk psychology.

Conclusions

Pinker (forthcoming) argues that the evolution of the human mind should be considered in terms of its ability to adapt to its environment. In his view, the brain needed to be able to maximize the survival of its host body in response to at least two broad challenges: the physical environment and the social environment. The specialized cognitive domains of folk physics and folk psychology can be seen as adaptations to each of these environments.

One possibility is that a cognitive profile that includes superior folk physics alongside impaired folk psychology could arise for genetic reasons, in that some brains are better adapted to understanding the physical environment while other brains are better adapted to understanding the social environment. The "male brain" may be an instance of the former, and the "female brain" an instance of the latter, given the evidence from experimental studies of sex differences (Halpern, 1982). In this view, the autistic brain may be an extreme form of the male brain (Baron-Cohen and Hammer, "Is Autism and Extreme Form of the Male Brain?" forthcoming).

The human brain can be construed as a causation-focused cognitive machine that searches for both intentional and physical causes underlying observable events. By this account, if a brain has a genetic-based impairment in folk psychology, this will cause that brain to spend less time interacting with the social environment and more time interacting with the physical environment, since at least it can understand the latter. A simple mass-practice or expertise model could then explain why such a brain, developing along an

Table 3.1. Percentage of Fathers and Grandfathers of Children With and Without Autism in Two Contrasting Occupations

	Engineering	Social Work
Fathers of children with autism	12.5	2.6
Grandfathers of children with autism	10.6	0.5
Fathers of children without autism	5.6	5.0
Grandfathers of children without autism	5.0	2.5

abnormally one-sided trajectory, could end up showing a superiority in folk physics.

What is the extra explanatory scope that this account provides, over and above the (now standard) theory of mind account of autism? The theory of mind account has been virtually silent on why children with autism should show repetitive behavior, a strong desire for routines, and a need for sameness. To date the only cognitive theory that has attempted to explain this aspect of the syndrome is the executive dysfunction theory (Ozonoff, Rogers, Farnham; and Pennington, 1994; Pennington and others, forthcoming; Russell, 1996). This paints an essentially negative view of this behavior, one that assumes that it is a form of "frontal lobe" perseveration or an inability to shift attention.

Although some forms of low-level repetitive behavior in autistics, such as stereotypies (for example, twiddling the fingers rapidly in peripheral vision) may be due to executive deficits or understimulation, the executive dysfunction account has traditionally ignored the *content* of repetitive behavior. The theory outlined in this chapter draws attention to the fact that much repetitive behavior involves autistic children's "obsessional" or strong interests in mechanical systems (such as light switches and water faucets) or other systems that can be understood in physical-causal terms. (The term *obsession* can only be used with difficulty in the context of autism [Baron-Cohen, 1989b]. Although obsessions are traditionally defined as "egodystonic," or unwanted, there is no evidence that an autistic's strong interests are unwanted. Rather, they appear to provide some pleasure and are therefore probably egosyntonic.) Rather than being a sign of executive dysfunction, these behaviors may reflect autistic children's intact or even superior development of folk physics. Autistic children's "obsession" with machines and systems, and what is often described as their "need for sameness" in attempting to hold their environment constant, might be signs that autistics are superior folk physicists, conducting miniexperiments in their surroundings in an attempt to identify physical-causal principles underlying events.

In summary, the argument advanced here is that the brain basically has only two modes of causal cognition: a folk psychology and a folk physics. In the most extreme case, severe autism may be characterized by almost no folk psychology (and thus "mindblindness"). But just as cases of autism and AS vary in degree, so might different points on the autistic spectrum involve different degrees of deficits in folk psychology. For those autistic children who have no accompanying mental handicap (that is, those whose intelligence is in the normal range), their folk physics will develop not only normally but at a superior level. This could be the result of both a genetic liability and the development of expertise in nonsocial learning environments. There is every reason to expect that individuals with this sort of cognitive profile would have been selected for in hominid evolution, since good folk physics confers important advantages (such as tool use, construction, and so on). Indeed, it is a tautology that without highly developed folk physics (for example, engineering), Homo sapiens would still be preindustrial.

References

Bailey, S., and others. "Autism as a Strongly Genetic Disorder: Evidence from a British Twin Study." *Psychological Medicine,* 1995, *25,* 63–77.

Baillargeon, R., Kotovsky, L., and Needham, A. "The Acquisition of Physical Knowledge in Infancy." In D. Sperber, D. Premack, and A. Premack (eds.), *Causal Cognition: A Multidisciplinary Debate.* New York: Oxford University Press, 1995.

Baron-Cohen, S. "Autism and Symbolic Play." *British Journal of Developmental Psychology,* 1987, *5,* 139–148.

Baron-Cohen, S. "Social and Pragmatic Deficits in Autism: Cognitive or Affective?" *Journal of Autism and Developmental Disorders,* 1988, *18,* 379–402.

Baron-Cohen, S. "Are Autistic Children Behaviourists? An Examination of Their Mental-Physical and Appearance-Reality Distinctions." *Journal of Autism and Developmental Disorders,* 1989a, *19,* 579–600.

Baron-Cohen, S. "Do Autistic Children Have Obsessions and Compulsions?" *British Journal of Clinical Psychology,* 1989b, *28,* 193–200.

Baron-Cohen, S. "How to Build a Baby That Can Read Minds: Cognitive Mechanisms in Mindreading." *Cahiers de Psychologie Cognitive* [Current Psychology of Cognition], 1994, *13,* 513–552.

Baron-Cohen, S. *Mindblindness: An Essay on Autism and Theory of Mind.* Cambridge, Mass.: Bradford Books, 1995.

Baron-Cohen, S., and Goodhart, F. "The 'Seeing Leads to Knowing' Deficit in Autism: The Pratt and Bryant Probe." *British Journal of Developmental Psychology,* 1994, *12,* 397–402.

Baron-Cohen, S., and Hammer, J. "Is Autism an Extreme Form of the Male Brain?" *Advances in Infant Behaviour and Development,* forthcoming.

Baron-Cohen, S., and Hammer, J. "Parents of Children with Asperger Syndrome: What Is the Cognitive Phenotype?" *Journal of Cognitive Neuroscience,* forthcoming.

Baron-Cohen, S., Jolliffe, T., Mortimore, C., and Robertson, M. "An Even More Advanced Test of Theory of Mind: Evidence from Very High Functioning Adults with Autism or Asperger Syndrome." *Journal of Child Psychology and Psychiatry,* forthcoming.

Baron-Cohen, S., Leslie, A. M., and Frith, U. "Does the Autistic Child Have a 'Theory of Mind'?" *Cognition,* 1985, *21,* 37–46.

Baron-Cohen, S., Leslie, A. M., and Frith, U. "Mechanical, Behavioural and Intentional Understanding of Picture Stories in Autistic Children." *British Journal of Developmental Psychology,* 1986, *4,* 113–125.

Baron-Cohen, S., Tager-Flusberg, H., and Cohen, D. (eds.). *Understanding Other Minds: Perspectives from Autism.* New York: Oxford University Press, 1993.

Baron-Cohen, S., and others. "Is There a Link Between Engineering and Autism?" *Autism: An International Journal of Research and Practice,* forthcoming.

Bettelheim, B. *The Empty Fortress.* New York: Free Press, 1968.

Bolton, P., and others. "A Case-Control Family History Study of Autism." *Journal of Child Psychology and Psychiatry,* 1994, *35,* 877–900.

Brentano, F. von. *Psychology from an Empirical Standpoint.* New York: Routledge, 1970. (Originally published 1874.)

Carey, S. *Conceptual Change in Childhood.* Cambridge, Mass.: Bradford Books, 1985.

Charman, T., and Baron-Cohen, S. "Understanding Beliefs and Drawings: A Further Test of the Metarepresentation Theory of Autism." *Journal of Child Psychology and Psychiatry,* 1992, *33,* 1105–1112.

Charman, T., and Baron-Cohen, S. "Understanding Models, Photos, and Beliefs: A Test of the Modularity Thesis of Metarepresentation." *Cognitive Development,* 1995, *10,* 287–298.

Dennett, D. *Brainstorms: Philosophical Essays on Mind and Psychology.* Sussex, England: Harvester, 1978.

Folstein, S., and Rutter, M. "Infantile Autism: A Genetic Study of 21 Twin Pairs." *Journal of Child Psychology and Psychiatry,* 1977, *18,* 297–321.

Gergely, G., Nadasdy, Z., Gergely, C., and Biro, S. "Taking the Intentional Stance at 12 Months of Age." *Cognition,* 1995, *56,* 165–193.

Halpern, J. *Sex Differences in Cognition.* Hillsdale, N.J.: Erlbaum, 1982.

Hart, C. *Without Reason.* New York: HarperCollins, 1989.

Heider, F., and Simmel, M. "An Experimental Study of Apparent Behaviour." *American Journal of Psychology,* 1944, *57,* 243–259.

Jolliffe, T., and Baron-Cohen, S. "Are Adults with Autism or Asperger's Syndrome Faster Than Normal on the Embedded Figures Task?" *Journal of Child Psychology and Psychiatry,* forthcoming.

Le Couteur, A., and others. "A Broader Phenotype of Autism: The Clinical Spectrum in Twins." *Journal of Child Psychology and Psychiatry,* 1996, *37,* 785–801.

Leekam, S., and Perner, J. "Does the Autistic Child Have a Metarepresentational Deficit?" *Cognition,* 1991, *40,* 203–218.

Leslie, A. M. "ToMM, ToBy, and Agency: Core Architecture and Domain Specificity." In L. Hirschfeld and S. Gelman (eds.), *Domain Specificity in Cognition and Culture.* New York: Cambridge University Press, 1995.

Leslie, A. M., and Keeble, S. "Do Six-Month-Old Infants Perceive Causality?" *Cognition,* 1987, *25,* 265–288.

Leslie, A. M., and Thaiss, L. "Domain Specificity in Conceptual Development: Evidence from Autism." *Cognition,* 1992, *43,* 225–251.

Lovell, A. *In a Summer Garment.* London: Secker & Warburg, 1978.

Morton, J., Frith, U., and Leslie, A. "The Cognitive Basis of a Biological Disorder: Autism." *Trends in Neurosciences,* 1991, *14,* 434–438.

Ozonoff, S., Rogers, S., Farnham, J., and Pennington, B. "Can Standard Measures Identify Subclinical Markers of Autism?" *Journal of Autism and Developmental Disorders,* 1994, *23,* 429–441.

Park, C. *The Siege.* London: Hutchinson, 1967.

Pennington, B., and others. "Validity Test of the Executive Dysfunction Hypothesis of Autism." In J. Russell (ed.), *Executive Functioning in Autism.* Oxford, England: Oxford University Press, forthcoming.

Pinker, S. *How the Mind Works.* Harmondsworth, England: forthcoming.

Premack, D. "Do Infants Have a Theory of Self-Propelled Objects?" *Cognition,* 1990, *36,* 1–16.

Russell, J. (ed.). *Agency: Its Role in Mental Development.* Hillsdale, N.J.: Erlbaum, 1996.

Shah, A., and Frith, U. "An Islet of Ability in Autism: A Research Note." *Journal of Child Psychology and Psychiatry,* 1983, *24,* 613–620.

Sigman, M., Ungerer, J., Mundy, P., and Sherman, T. "Cognition in Autistic Children." In D. Cohen and A. Donnellan (eds.), *Handbook of Autism and Pervasive Developmental Disorders.* New York: Wiley, 1987.

Spelke, E., Phillips, A., and Woodward, A. "Infants' Knowledge of Object Motion and Human Action." In D. Sperber, D. Premack, and A. J. Premack (eds.), *Causal Cognition: A Multi-disciplinary Debate.* New York: Oxford University Press, 1995.

Sperber, D., Premack, D., and Premack, A. J. (eds.). *Causal Cognition: A Multi-disciplinary Debate.* New York: Oxford University Press, 1995.

Wimmer, H., and Perner, J. "Beliefs About Beliefs: Representation and Constraining Function of Wrong Beliefs in Young Children's Understanding of Deception." *Cognition,* 1983, *13,* 103–128.

SIMON BARON-COHEN is university lecturer in psychopathology, University of Cambridge, and fellow at Trinity College, Cambridge, England.

Signing deaf children who grow up in hearing homes without a fluently signing family member show a selective impairment in theory of mind. Deaf children who grow up with a fluent signer, however, display normal patterns of development in the psychological domain.

Domain Specificity and Everyday Biological, Physical, and Psychological Thinking in Normal, Autistic, and Deaf Children

Candida C. Peterson, Michael Siegal

Children's cognitive development can be described as the growth of a set of core understandings, or naive theories, in domains of knowledge such as biology, physics, and psychology (Wellman and Gelman, 1992). As they progressively observe and experiment with the animate and inanimate items in the world around them, children may reflect on their experience, question and converse with others, and refine their ideas systematically so as to gain everyday understandings within specific knowledge domains. For example, a focus on how to predict and influence the behavior of important people in his or her life may lead the child to develop a naive psychology, including theorizing about the human mind. A preoccupation with the structure and functioning of useful objects like toys and tools may lead to a naive theory of physics, including an understanding of how mechanical devices like cameras can represent information. Observations of the birth and growth of pets, the cultivation of plants, and other interactions with the world of nature may give rise to a naive biology, including notions of the roles of heredity and environment in shaping family resemblances.

This research was supported by a grant from the Australian Research Council. We wish to thank Helen Bosisto, Gayle Follett, Margaret Gore, Alexa Hinze, Pam Jokic, Wendy Newman, and James Peterson for their assistance with data collection, and all the children who took part, their parents, and their teachers for their fine cooperation.

Background

The study of how these naive theories are constructed by children with serious sensory, cognitive, linguistic, or social disabilities can help in understanding the development of both normal and handicapped children. For example, a large body of research confirms that autistic children are significantly delayed in acquiring a theory of mind (Baron-Cohen, Leslie, and Frith, 1985; Baron-Cohen, 1988). In particular, autistic children and adolescents are likely even at advanced mental ages to fail false-belief tests passed by most normal children by age four. Yet, somewhat paradoxically, these same young people with autism frequently succeed at other tasks requiring an understanding of photographic representation (Leekam and Perner, 1991; Leslie and Thaiss, 1992), of visual perception (Reed and Peterson, 1990), and of simple emotions and desires (Baron-Cohen, 1991). Given that the general instructions and procedures for these tasks resemble those for false-belief tests, such findings suggest that the cognitive deficit in autism is confined to concepts of mind.

According to Frith, Happe, and Siddons (1994, p. 110), "In the normally developing child the computational capacity to represent mental states has an innate neurological basis. In the autistic child, neurological damage to a circumscribed system of the brain has occurred." If the damage is caused by the unique set of factors that gives rise to a diagnosis of autism, then other groups of children with cognitive and developmental difficulties of a different etiology than those of children with autism would be expected to develop a theory of mind at approximately the same mental age as normal children. Support for this view has emerged for mentally retarded individuals (Baron-Cohen, 1988), those with emotional disturbances (Siddons, Happe, Whyte, and Frith, 1990), and those with expressive language disorders.

Yet the concept of damage to a circumscribed system of the brain is harder to reconcile with the discovery that signing profoundly deaf children with no cognitive, physical, or socioemotional impairments apart from deafness share autistic children's difficulties with theory of mind tasks (Deleau, forthcoming; Peterson and Siegal, 1995). Although deaf and autistic children may perform similarly on tests of a theory of mind for different reasons, they often do have a common set of social experiences that are not shared either by normally developing children or by those with mental retardation or speech disorders. The autistic child's social aloofness, in conjunction with his or her impaired communication and imagination (Frith, 1989), limits the child's opportunities to participate in conversation. In addition, longitudinal studies of spontaneous dialogues between mothers and their autistic children have revealed that talk about mental states is notably absent, as compared with families of Down's syndrome children (Tager-Flusberg, 1992). Profoundly deaf children who grow up in hearing homes where no one uses sign language with the same fluency as a native signer often have similar problems participating in conversations, and like autistic children they may be selectively cut off from talk about intangible topics like thoughts and beliefs. Power and Carty (1990) found that deaf native signers of Australian sign language (Auslan) generally experienced impoverished early communication in the family setting and did not acquire a fluent conversational medium until joining other deaf pupils in primary school. Meadow, Greenberg, Erting, and Carmichael (1981) compared deaf preschool children of hearing and signing parents. Those whose parents were hearing had great difficulty carrying on conversations about themselves, their mothers, and nonpresent objects or events, even when their parents had made considerable effort to learn sign language. But the deaf preschoolers who had deaf parents conversed as fluently in sign as did preschoolers of normal hearing in speech.

Results like these suggest an alternative to the nativist neurological account of the normal growth of a theory of mind. At least two crucial functions in cognitive development may be served by spontaneous family discussions of thoughts, desires, mistaken beliefs, or fantasy play. First, in line with Brown, Donelan-McCall, and Dunn's report (1996) that fluent use of mental state terms in hearing three-year-olds' spontaneous conversations with their siblings and friends is linked both with cooperative play and with success on standard false-belief tasks, dialogues like these may stimulate a child's reasoning about the human mind and provide exposure to the ways in which his or her own beliefs and those of others guide behavior. Second, a rich early exposure to varied conversation may equip normal children with the pragmatic communication skills necessary to follow the conversational implications of theory of mind tasks. In such tasks, for example, children are required to recognize that the purpose and relevance of an experimenter's questioning is to determine where a character with a false belief will mistakenly search for an object and to block out the competing implication that the purpose in questioning is to identify where the character will have to search to retrieve the object successfully (Siegal, 1997; Siegal and Beattie, 1991; Siegal and Peterson, 1994). In this connection, considerable research has now shown that success on standard false-belief tests is dependent upon a certain level of linguistic skill (Jenkins and Astington, 1996).

These considerations suggest that conversational deprivation could selectively disadvantage both autistic children and deaf children from hearing families, not only in terms of access to core knowledge about thoughts and beliefs but also in terms of test performance.

The Study

One way to clarify whether deaf and autistic children's comparable difficulties with theory of mind tasks have a common or a disparate origin is to explore further similarities and differences between these groups in core domains of knowledge. In this respect, a major aim of the study reported here was to compare the performance of deaf children who had the conversational advantage of exposure to fluently signing deaf family members with those whose early conversational access was limited to hearing parents and siblings who could not converse in sign as fluently as native signers. We chose to examine three domains of knowledge: psychological, physical, and biological. According to Wellman and Gelman (1992), an understanding of how children develop mental models of these conceptual domains is likely to have important theoretical implications. As these three areas of knowledge span the breadth of everyday life, and "as it is hard to imagine any more fundamental cognitive tasks than knowing about people, about plants and animals and about the world of objects" (Wellman and Gelman, 1992, p. 342), their process of mastery provides insight into cognitive development at its broadest level.

A second aim of our study was to compare conversationally normal and conversationally handicapped children's rates of development across domains, to explore whether thinking develops independently within each domain or is connected from one domain to the next. If cognitive development is domain-general, acceleration in one domain should predict early mastery over others. But if development is domain-specific, performance on similarly structured conceptual problems taken from each domain should emerge as relatively independent, both in normal children and in children with early conversational deprivation. To the extent that conversational experience assists either with acquisition of a core domain of knowledge (Peterson and Siegal, 1995) or with a child's capacity to display such knowledge in experimental tasks (Leslie, 1994; Siegal and Beattie, 1991), autistic children and deaf children from hearing families are likely to demonstrate understanding of that domain more slowly than children with a richer early exposure to conversation. However, if knowledge in a given domain develops largely without the aid of verbal social interaction, then groups of conversationally deprived deaf and autistic children should master tasks from that domain at a normal rate, provided the tasks are structured in a manner that minimizes the need to follow complex pragmatic or conversational implications (Siegal, 1997).

Parallel to false-belief tasks in which children are required to focus on the believed location of an object rather than its more salient real location, we chose tasks from the domains of physics and biology that required an awareness of the continuity of implicit or inferential cues, despite salient changes in the visible external environment. To characterize the physical domain, we used the specific task of reasoning about cameras and false photographs (physical representations that are at odds with reality). Here previous research suggests that autistic children (Leekam and Perner, 1991; Leslie and Thaiss, 1992) and deaf children from hearing families (Peterson and Siegal, 1997) may perform more competently than would be predicted by their delayed grasp of false belief (mental representations that are at odds with reality).

To investigate reasoning in the domain of biology, we examined children's implicit notions of "something like genetics" (Gelman and Wellman, 1991, p. 239). These notions are embodied in an accurate recognition of the continuity from parent to offspring of physical characteristics that distinguish members of one species from other species sharing the same rearing environment (Springer and Keil, 1989). An early understanding of biologically encoded information or inherent "essence" allows children to make accurate predictions of developmental outcomes in adoption or transplantation situations. In the tasks used in our study, the former depicted animals born to one species but reared by another, whereas the latter depicted seeds extracted from one kind of plant but growing in the midst of others. To succeed on each task, the child had to recognize the essential continuity of invisible species characteristics transmitted biologically to offspring, while ignoring salient information about the visible rearing environment.

We predicted that autistic children and signing deaf children from hearing families would display more problems than normal preschoolers with theory of mind tasks, owing to their early deprivation of conversational experience and their selective lack of exposure to talk about other people's covert mental states (Peterson and Siegal, 1995). By contrast, we expected that those signing deaf children who had grown up in a family with a fluently signing conversational partner would show normal patterns of development in the psychological domain as a result of their ready access to at least one individual with whom they could share thoughts, beliefs, and other varied modes of conversation from an early age.

When it came to tasks taken from the domains of physics and biology, we did not predict differences among diagnostic groups. With regard to false photographs, deaf children in hearing homes and socially aloof autistic children are likely to gain normal access to cameras and might even be expected to understand their mechanics at an earlier-than-normal age, owing to an intrinsic interest in such devices and the largely visual nature of the conjectures necessary to comprehend this sort of mechanical functioning. With regard to biological understanding, we anticipated that older deaf and autistic children would have had at least as much involvement as normal four-year-olds in cultivating seeds and rearing pets (Inagaki, 1990) and so would do as well as normal preschoolers on the biological tasks. Similarly, we predicted no differences on biological or physics tasks as a function of deaf children's exposure to sign language in the family.

Methods, Procedures, and Experimental Tasks

The participants in this research were ninety-nine Australian children in two separate samples, ranging in age from three years nine months to fourteen years eight months. Sample 1 consisted of sixty-eight children: sixteen had autism, nineteen were deaf, and the remainder were normal four-year-olds recruited from preschools and day-care centers serving predominantly middle-class Brisbane, Australia, neighborhoods. Sample 2, tested one year later, consisted of sixteen deaf children and fifteen normal preschoolers.

The sixteen able autistic subjects (fifteen boys and one girl) who remained in Sample 1 after the exclusion of four who failed control questions (three false-belief, one false-photo) had a mean chronological age of nine years eight months (ranging from four years six months to fourteen years eight months), and all had a verbal mental age of four years or higher on the Peabody Picture Vocabulary Test. They had all been diagnosed as autistic according to DSM III-R criteria and were attending a special school for autism. The nineteen signing severely and profoundly deaf children in Sample 1 (eleven boys and eight girls) were pupils in Total Communication units attached to state-supported primary schools. Their mean age was eight years eleven months (ranging from four years ten months to thirteen years three months), and none of them had any known or suspected physical, intellectual, or social handicaps apart from hearing loss. All of these deaf children were fluent users of signed or manual communication (including facets of signed English and Auslan, plus finger spelling), and this was their predominant mode of interacting with their teachers and deaf classmates. However, their background exposure to sign language differed. Five of these signing deaf children (26 percent of Sample 1) were dubbed "native signers" because they had grown up in a household with a fluently signing deaf family member (a parent, grandparent, or sibling). They had a mean age of nine years ten months (ranging from seven years nine months to eleven years six months). The remaining fourteen deaf children had grown up in exclusively hearing homes where no other family member was as fluent in sign language as a native speaker. Thus their exposure to manual communication had been of shorter duration, often coinciding with entry into primary school. In addition, Sample 1 contained thirty-three normal preschoolers in two subgroups. Group A included twenty-two children (thirteen boys and nine girls) with a mean age of four years nine months (ranging from four years seven months to five years five months) who completed the belief, photo, and original biology tasks. After the exclusion of one child who failed a false-belief control question, Group B consisted of eleven normal preschoolers (four boys and seven girls) with a mean age of four years eleven months (ranging from four years one month to five years seven months) who completed the belief and photo tasks only.

Sample 2 contained thirty-one children. They had backgrounds similar to the children in Sample 1, but none of them had previously been tested. The fifteen normal preschoolers (seven boys and eight girls) in Group C had a mean age of four years four months (ranging from three years nine months to four years ten months). The sixteen deaf children in Sample 2 (eight boys and eight girls) had a mean age of ten years one month (ranging from six years four months to twelve years eight months). There were four native signers in this group, with a mean age of eleven years (ranging from eight years eight months to twelve years eight months), as well as twelve deaf children who had grown up in exclusively hearing families. All Sample 2 children completed the false-belief and modified biological tasks.

Each deaf child was tested individually by two adults, the male experimenter (E) and a professionally trained Auslan interpreter who was highly familiar with the styles of Total Communication used in each classroom and with each child's own particular language preferences (for example, for signed English versus Auslan) and who used this favored form of sign language to translate tasks and questions. Both adults independently recorded the child's pointing responses, and subsequent matching of their records revealed complete agreement. In addition, the interpreter supplied an ongoing oral translation of all the child's signed communications, which were then recorded in writing. The autistic children were also tested by the same male experimenter, plus a different, female assistant who independently recorded the children's responses. The normal preschoolers were tested individually by a single female experimenter.

False-Belief Task. Baron-Cohen, Leslie, and Frith's "Sally/Anne" test of false belief (1985) was used exactly as described by those authors, except that a boy doll was substituted for their "Anne" to avoid the need for finger spelling and remembering of names. In brief, the procedure consisted of two trials, each beginning with the girl doll's hiding a marble in a basket and leaving the scene. While she was gone, the boy doll shifted the marble. The girl returned, and the subject was asked the test question: "Where will the girl look for her marble?" (correct answer: in the basket). This was followed by two control questions: "Where is the marble really?" and "Where did the girl put the marble in the beginning?" Correct responses to control questions established that subjects noticed the new location and remembered the original hiding place. Owing to the inherent ambiguity of drawing inferences about awareness of false belief from a child who misunderstood the experimental task, any subject who failed either of the control questions on either trial was excluded from the sample. The second trial was identical, apart from use of the experimenter's pocket as the hiding place. With three feasible locations, the odds of chance success on this trial through random guessing were only 33 percent. However, we adhered to Baron-Cohen, Leslie, and Frith's more stringent requirement (1985) that a subject must pass both test questions in order to be credited with an understanding of false belief (resulting in chance odds of 17 percent).

False-Photo Task. This task was closely based on Zaitchik's false-photograph task (1990). Materials consisted of a Polaroid camera, a Duplo mother and baby doll, and a set of Duplo infant furniture. Each child was pretrained in the use of the camera and coached to see the development of a practice photo to completion, as described by Zaitchik (1990). The experimenter then said, "Here is the baby. Sometimes the baby is in the bath" (demonstration). "Sometimes the baby is in the bed" (demonstration). "Sometimes the baby is in the pram" (demonstration). "Now let's put the baby in the bath. Let's take a photo of the baby in the bath. Can you see the baby in the bath through the little window? Okay, press the button. We wait a minute for the photo" (Polaroid snapshot goes face down on desk). "Here comes Mum. She takes the baby out of the bath and puts him in bed. Now I'll ask you some questions":

Test question: "In the photo, where is the baby?"
Memory control question: "Where was the baby when the camera flashed?"
Reality control question: "Where is the baby now?"

The furniture items and the order of the demonstrations varied. With three possible locations to choose from, the odds of chance success on the test question were 33 percent.

Biology Task 1 (Seeds). This task questioned children about transplanted seeds. The storybook procedure was adapted from Gelman and Wellman's Study 5 (1991). The experimenter said, "This is a seed from a [watermelon]" while showing a life-sized picture of the seed and a cut fruit. Next came a picture of a planting environment (such as a grove of orange trees laden with oranges). There was also a small centrally placed hole, to which the experimenter pointed, saying, "We plant the seed in a [grove where oranges are growing]. The seed grows and grows under the ground. Now it is going to sprout up out of the ground." Three questions followed with both pictures still visible:

Test question: "When the seed sprouts up, what will it be?"
Memory control question: "What [fruit/plant] did the seed come from?"
Reality control question: "What [fruits/plants] are growing all around where the seed was planted?"

The procedure was then repeated in full with a new story, so that each child completed two trials. There were a number of versions of the task, each involving different plants of origin (watermelon, flower, peach, orange, avocado) and different plants in the growing environment (cactuses, flowers, orange trees, pineapples, or coconut palms). Teachers were consulted in advance of the experiment to select versions involving plants familiar to most of their class. Children always received different plants in each situation on each trial. If a child failed either control question on the initial presentation, that trial was discarded and the task was presented again later in the experimental sequence, usually on a different day. More than one control-question failure was scored as failure of the task as a whole, but we did not drop these children from the overall sample.

Biology Task 2 (Animals). This task involved animals born to one species and reared by another. There were two versions, one original and one modified. Both were adapted from Gelman and Wellman's Study 3 (1991). However, we removed these authors' species labels (for example, "When she was a tiny baby cow . . .") in favor of human names (such as "Edith"), and the baby animals in our stories were pictured only in a nondescript, embryonic way that had been carefully piloted with adults to remove any visual suggestion of membership within either relevant species. Small and larger versions of these round, pink, embryolike creatures appeared on facing pages of the storybook, accompanied by realistic pictures of the parent animals. Pointing at the first picture, the experimenter said, "This is a picture of a baby animal. Her name is Edith. This is her mother the [cat]. When she was still a tiny baby, Edith went to live with a family of [dogs]. Here is the mother [dog] and father [dog], who raised her like their own baby. She lived with these [dogs] all her life until she was grown up, and she never saw a [cat] again. Now Edith is all grown up." Three questions followed:

Test question 1: "Which of these is a picture of Edith now that she is grown up?" (Pictures of a cat and dog were placed on the table in a counterbalanced position.)

Test question 2: "What kind of animal is Edith now that she is grown up?" (If there was no response, E prompted, "Is she a cat or a dog?")

Memory control question: "Point to the animals who gave birth to Edith" (If there was no response, "Show me her mother when she was born.")

Reality control question: "Who raised Edith?" (If there was no response, "Who did she live with all her life?")

There were two versions, one with cats as the birth species and dogs as the rearing species, the other vice versa. A preliminary analysis revealed no significant effects related to the different versions, so data from both were combined. Children passed if they replied correctly to both test questions and all four control questions. Those who failed any control questions failed the task but were retained in the sample.

For Sample 2 we created a modified task in which a baby animal named Edgar was born to lions and reared by zebras. Pictures of the same embryonic creatures with accurate drawings of both sets of parent animals were used, and the second test question was modified to, "Is Edgar a lion or a zebra?" [counterbalance: a zebra or a lion]. The remainder of the procedure and scoring was the same as for Sample 1.

Results

Table 4.1 shows the percentages and numbers of children passing selected tasks as a function of diagnostic group.

Theory of Mind. Preliminary analyses revealed no statistically significant difference between the 80 percent of deaf native signers who passed the false-belief task in Sample 1 and the 100 percent of Sample 2 who did so, $p > .20$, Fisher's exact probability test. Nor was there a significant difference between the 57 and 33 percent, respectively, of signing deaf children from hearing families in the two samples who passed, $\chi^2(1) = 1.47$, $N = 26$, $p > .10$. The three subgroups of normal preschoolers likewise displayed equivalently high rates of success, $\chi^2(2) < 1$, $N = 48$, $p > .20$. Thus the combined data of children from the same diagnostic category across the two samples, as shown in Table 4.1, were used for further analyses involving false belief.

When the performance of the autistic group, the normal preschool group, the deaf native signers, and the signing deaf children from hearing families was contrasted on the false-belief task, a statistically significant difference emerged among the diagnostic groups, $\chi^2(3) = 8.55$, $N = 99$, $p < .05$, two-tailed. The deaf children from hearing families performed no better than the autistic

Table 4.1. Percentages and Numbers of Children Passing Tasks from Three Domains

Domain: Task:	Psychological False-Belief	Physical False-Photo	Biological	
			Seeds	Animals*
Group:				
Deaf native signers	89%	100%	44%	75%
	(8/9)	(5/5)	(4/9)	(3/4)
Deaf from hearing families	46%	79%	65%	67%
	(12/26)	(11/14)	(17/26)	(8/12)
Autistic children	44%	88%	63%	81%
	(7/16)	(14/16)	(10/16)	(13/16)
Normal preschoolers	69%	100%	78%	84%
	(33/48)	(33/33)	(29/37)	(31/37)

*Based on original task for autistic group, modified task for deaf groups, and both tasks for normal preschoolers.

children, $\chi^2(1) < 1$, $N = 42$, $p > .20$. However, there was a significant difference between the two deaf groups, $\chi^2(1) = 4.99$, $N = 35$, $p < .05$, two-tailed. Significantly more of those with a signing deaf relative passed (89 percent) than did those from hearing families (46 percent). Similarly, when we combined the autistic children with the deaf children from hearing families, to create a group of conversationally deprived children, this group failed the false-belief test more often than the normal preschoolers, $\chi^2(1) = 5.08$, $N = 90$, $p < .05$, two-tailed, and more often than the native-signer deaf children, $\chi^2(1) = 5.69$, $N = 51$, $p < .02$, two-tailed. These findings support previous research (Peterson and Siegal, 1997) by indicating that, unless signing deaf children grow up in a family with a signing deaf relative, they are likely to have as much difficulty with theory of mind tasks as autistic children at similarly advanced mental ages.

False Photographic Representation. As shown in Table 4.1, all groups displayed a very adept understanding of false photographic representation, with the vast majority of children in each diagnostic category passing. Indeed, the normal preschoolers and the deaf native signers displayed perfect performance, and the autistic group, like the signing deaf children from hearing families, achieved a significantly higher level of success than the 33 percent to be expected by chance ($z = 4.42$ and 3.36, respectively, $p < .01$ for both, two-tailed).

Biological Understanding. A comparison of deaf children's performance on the original versus the modified animals task revealed that the latter resulted in a significantly higher rate of success, $\chi^2(1) = 4.81$, $N = 35$, $p < .05$, supporting the possibility that either one of two methodological artifacts may have selectively impaired the deaf children's comprehension of the original version. One involved the wording of Sample 1's test question: "What kind of animal is Edith?" According to Gregory, Bishop, and Sheldon (1995), the use of *kind* in this context can prove problematic when translated into sign language. In their interview schedule, administered with the aid of a fluently signing deaf interpreter to a group of deaf British adults from a signing background similar to that of the present deaf group, the question "What kind of person are you?" was frequently misinterpreted. Deaf adults often replied, "Yes, I am a kind person." The possibility that some signers in Sample 1 may similarly have misinterpreted our test question, thinking we were asking about the animal's kindness rather than her species, was reinforced by the post hoc observation that five of the six who failed only one test question had pointed to the correct animal's picture while erring when asked about its "kind." Thus this question was rephrased for Sample 2, as described previously under "Method." Secondly, use of cats and dogs as contrasting species may have proved problematic for some deaf children. Deaf children are cut off from the distinctive auditory cues that unequivocally distinguish meowing cats from barking dogs for normal children. In spite of obvious cross-species visual differences (even for similar-sized animals such as a Chihuahua versus a cat), the deaf children may not have perceived the species boundary between these two particular types of household pet as clearly as did hearing children. Thus the clearly distinctive yet familiar species of lions and zebras were substituted for cats and dogs in the modified task.

The normal preschoolers did as well on the original task as the modified one, $\chi^2(1) < 1$, so we combined the two normal samples but used only the Sample 2 deaf children in a comparison of performance on the animals task by the diagnostic groups. No statistically significant difference emerged, $\chi^2(2) = 1.63$, $N = 69$, $p > .50$, and all groups scored significantly above the 25 percent level of success that would be expected through chance guessing ($z = 3.80$, 4.91 and 8.29 for deaf, autistic, and normal children, respectively, $p < .01$ for each).

Seeds Task. Since the same format and question wording was used for this task with both samples, we conducted preliminary analyses to establish comparability of Samples 1 and 2. No significant difference emerged by Fisher's exact probability test between the 40 percent of deaf native signers from Sample 1 who passed and the 50 percent from Sample 2 who passed. There were similarly no significant differences in the success rates for deaf children from hearing families or between the two samples of normal four-year-olds, χ^2s < 1 for both. Thus combined data from the two samples, shown in Table 4.1, were used in testing for diagnostic group differences. The result was not statistically significant, $\chi^2(3) = 1.71$, $N = 88$, $p > .50$. Furthermore, the preschoolers ($z = 5.27$, $p < .01$), the autistic children ($z = 3.24$, $p < .01$), and the combined group of native signers and nonnative signers ($z = 3.80$, $p < .01$) were each more successful on the two combined trials of the seeds task than the 25 percent that would expected from random guessing.

Associations Between Domains. As noted earlier, a domain-general model of development predicts that early mastery of a theory of mind should be linked with early mastery of salient phenomena in other domains. We therefore examined the extent to which success on our false-belief task predicted success on the tests of photographic representation and biological inheritance.

A total of sixty-eight children took the false-photo test, and sixty-three of them (93 percent) passed it. There was no statistically significant difference between the 95 percent success rate on the false-photo task by those who understood false belief and the 88 percent success rate by those who did not, $\chi^2(1) = 1.24, N = 68, p > .20$.

Before comparing children's biological and psychological understanding, we checked the feasibility of combining the two biological tasks. Each child was given a score of 0, 1, or 2 on each of the tasks, reflecting the number of correct answers they had given to test questions on trials for which they had also correctly answered control questions. When accuracy on the seeds and animals tasks was correlated, a statistically significant relationship emerged, r (67) $= .24, p < .05$, two-tailed. In other words, the two tasks appeared to reliably measure a common dimension of biological understanding. We therefore assigned combined biological knowledge scores of 0, 1, or 2, reflecting the total number of biology tasks (seeds, animals, or both) that each child had passed. These scores were analyzed in a 2 (pass-fail false-belief) $\times$ 3 (diagnostic group) ANOVA, with deaf children from Sample 2 only and the native and nonnative signers combined. No statistically significant main effects emerged for diagnostic group ($F < 1$), for false-belief knowledge ($F < 1$), or for the interaction between these variables ($F < 1$). In other words, these results supported our earlier finding that conversationally deprived children did not lag behind conversationally normal children in mastery of biological concepts. Furthermore, there was no evidence in these data that acquisition of a theory of mind assisted children's understanding of the biological transmission of species characteristics.

Conclusions

The results for the false-belief task that we chose from the psychological domain indicated that autistic children and deaf children from hearing families did not differ significantly in their performance but were more prone to fail than normal preschoolers who were an average of five years younger. These results are in line with those of previous studies of autistic children (for example, Baron-Cohen, Leslie, and Frith, 1985) and of deaf children (Deleau, forthcoming; Peterson and Siegal, 1995, 1997). However, the present findings extend earlier studies of false-belief understanding by deaf children in a novel way. The subgroup of severely and profoundly deaf children in our sample who had grown up in a household with a fluently signing deaf conversational partner outperformed the rest of their signing deaf classmates. Indeed, virtually all passed the false-belief task that most deaf children from hearing families failed. Since educational background and other social and life experiences, apart from early exposure to sign language, were quite similar for these two subgroups of deaf children, this finding points strongly to early conversational experience at home as a determining factor in the acquisition of a theory of mind. A deaf child growing up with a signing deaf family member has the same access to conversational input as do hearing toddlers and preschoolers (Marschark, 1993), even though the language medium may be Ameslan, Auslan, or signed English rather than speech.

By contrast, up to the point of entering a signing classroom at school, "a deaf child of hearing parents may have no native language in the sense of a code shared by many users" (Charrow and Fletcher, 1974, p. 463), and communication with hearing family members is typically "limited to topics with a visual reference" (Meadow, 1975, p. 489). Thus these children may be deprived of linguistic cues to other people's mental states during the potentially critical preschool period. Observational studies in hearing homes document an abrupt increase in references to mental states in mother-child dialogues around age three (Brown and Dunn, 1991), which is just before hearing children master the conversational implications needed to succeed on standard tests of false belief (Leslie, 1994; Siegal and Beattie, 1991). Using a similar methodology, Tager-Flusberg (1992, 1993) noted a dearth of mental-state references in spontaneous dialogues between mothers and their autistic children—in contrast to children with Down's syndrome, who conversed with their mothers about thoughts and beliefs at a normal rate for their mental age. These results suggest that retarded children may experience the same sort of conversational impetus to master false belief that we propose explains the contrast between native and nonnative deaf signers' performance on such tasks; they further suggest that children with autism may resemble deaf preschoolers in hearing households in that both groups are denied important conversational input.

The parallels between the cognitive development of autistic children and that of signing deaf children from hearing families were found to extend beyond the domain of naive psychology to include naive physics and naive biology as well. Neither group had any difficulty at all with the physical concept of false representation by a still camera, and they were comparable to normal preschoolers, and significantly better than chance, at attributing the physical characteristics of transplanted plants and adopted animals to biological inheritance rather than environmental nurturance. Possibly a physical knowledge of how cameras work and a biological understanding that the essence of a mature animal or plant derives from its parent or its seed may develop normally in conversationally deprived deaf and autistic children as a result of their direct personal experience with taking pictures, planting seeds, and rearing pets (Inagaki, 1990).

At a broader level, these findings for conversationally deprived and conversationally normal children are consistent with one another in showing a disjunction between cognitive development in the domain of naive psychology compared to the domains of naive physics and naive biology. The tasks we used to assess understanding in each domain were closely parallel to one another, both procedurally and in their requirement that a subject ignore immediately salient environmental information in favor of nonobvious previous information. Yet there was no significant tendency, either among normal preschoolers or among conversationally handicapped children, for success on the false-belief task to predict accurate knowledge of biology or mechanical representation. This is in line with the possibility that a child's knowledge of the everyday world develops in a domain-specific manner (Wellman and Gelman, 1992).

The relatively adept performance by the four-year-olds in our sample on the false-photo and biological inheritance tasks also warrants consideration in light of previous claims that such tasks, unlike false belief, are beyond the competencies of this age group. The fact that every one of the normal preschoolers we tested managed to pass our modified version of Zaitchik's false-photo task is inconsistent with her conclusion that "the preschooler has an even harder time reasoning about photos than beliefs" (1990, p. 60). Similarly, the fact that the preschoolers in our sample succeeded at a level that was clearly above chance in demonstrating an awareness of the biological bases for the mature physical characteristics of transplanted seeds and adopted animals is out of line with the conclusion by Solomon, Johnson, Zaitchik, and Carey (1996) that preschoolers possess little or no understanding of biological inheritance.

Too many differences exist between the procedures, analytical techniques, and sample characteristics of the children tested in our own and these previous studies to allow an unequivocal explanation of such discrepancies in results. An urgent priority for further research is to examine the nature of children's responses to tasks presented in various formats. In this regard our data suggest that conversational and contextual factors in the testing situation exert powerful influences over what children say. It is possible that the lengthy dialogues about "feeling hot and tired" that accompanied the Sesame Street puppets' pretense of taking photographs in Zaitchik's study may have limited children's appreciation that the relevance and purpose of the experimenter's questioning was to discover the extent of their understanding of photographic representation. Similarly, in Solomon and colleagues' study, children may have imported their own relevance to such features of the tasks as the magical properties of a fairy-tale world of kings and shepherds, or the loving and motherly nature of the adoptive parents, or the unfamiliar topics (rusting metal, animals' night vision, and so on) used in describing the story characters' discordant beliefs. Consequently, it is possible that their answers may not have reflected the true extent of their knowledge of biological inheritance. Indeed, the contrast in our own results between the deaf children's responses to the original and modified animals tasks indicates that even relatively minor changes to stimuli and question wording can exert a significant effect on children's performance.

Naive theories in the biological, psychological, and physical domains could conceivably be acquired on the basis of innate constraints, as suggested by Berlin's anthropological observation (1972) that everyday botanical and zoological categories and nomenclature are stable across human cultures throughout the world, notwithstanding the wide variations that exist among the specific plants and animals occupying any given culture's habitat. But the notion of innate constraints on learning is not incompatible with the idea that specific experiences are also necessary for development. The present findings strongly suggest that the role played by early conversational experience in the growth of a theory of mind is an important one. The opportunity to share thoughts, beliefs, desires, and fantasy play with at least one fluently signing conversational partner at home appears to protect deaf children from the specific deficits in theory of mind development that this and previous studies have revealed among autistic children and deaf children in households without a fluent signer. Such findings have implications also for the development of psychological understanding through conversational experience in normal children.

References

Baron-Cohen, S. "Social and Pragmatic Deficits in Autism: Cognitive or Affective?" *Journal of Autism and Developmental Disorders,* 1988, *18,* 379–402.

Baron-Cohen, S. "Do People with Autism Understand What Causes Emotion?" *Child Development,* 1991, *62,* 385–395.

Baron-Cohen, S., Leslie, A. M., and Frith, U. "Does the Autistic Child Have a 'Theory of Mind'?" *Cognition,* 1985, *21,* 37–46.

Berlin, D. "Speculations on the Growth of Ethnobiological Nomenclature." *Language and Society,* 1972, *1,* 63–98.

Brown, J. R., Donelan-McCall, N., and Dunn, J. "Why Talk About Mental States? The Significance of Children's Conversations with Friends, Siblings and Mothers." *Child Development,* 1996, *67,* 836–849.

Brown, J. R., and Dunn, J. " 'You Can Cry Mum': The Social and Developmental Implications of Talk About Internal States." *British Journal of Developmental Psychology,* 1991, *9,* 237–256.

Charrow, V., and Fletcher, J. "English as a Second Language for Deaf Children." *Developmental Psychology,* 1974, *10,* 463–470.

Deleau, M. "L'attribution d'etats mentaux chez des enfants sourds et entendants: Une approche du role de l'experience langagiere sur une Theorie de l'Esprit" [Deaf and Hearing Children's Attributions of Mental States: Approaching the Influence of Language Experience on Theory of Mind]. *Bulletin de Psychologie* [Bulletin of Psychology], forthcoming.

Frith, U. *Autism: Explaining the Enigma.* Oxford, England: Oxford University Press, 1989.

Frith, U., Happe, F., and Siddons, F. "Autism and the Theory of Mind in Everyday Life." *Social Development,* 1994, *3,* 108–123.

Gelman, S. A., and Wellman, H. M. "Insides and Essences: Early Understandings of the Nonobvious." *Cognition,* 1991, *38,* 213–244.

Gregory, S., Bishop, J., and Sheldon, L. *Deaf Young People and Their Families.* Cambridge, England: Cambridge University Press, 1995.

Inagaki, K. "The Effects of Raising Animals on Children's Biological Knowledge." *British Journal of Developmental Psychology,* 1990, *8,* 119–129.

Jenkins, J. M., and Astington, J. W. "Cognitive Factors and Family Structure Associated with Theory of Mind Development in Young Children." *Developmental Psychology,* 1996, *32,* 70–78.

Leekam, S. R., and Perner, J. "Do Autistic Children Have a Metarepresentational Deficit?" *Cognition,* 1991, *40,* 203–218.

Leslie, A. M. "Pretending and Believing: Issues in the Theory of ToMM." *Cognition,* 1994, *50,* 211–238.

Leslie, A. M., and Thaiss, L. "Domain Specificity in Conceptual Development: Neuropsy-chological Evidence from Autism." *Cognition,* 1992, *43,* 225–251.

Marschark, M. *Psychological Development of Deaf Children.* New York: Oxford University Press, 1993.

Meadow, K. P. "The Development of Deaf Children." In E. M. Hetherington (ed.), *Review of Child Development Research.* Vol. 5. Thousand Oaks, Calif.: Sage, 1975.

Meadow, K. P., Greenberg, M. T., Erting, C., and Carmichael, H. "Interactions of Deaf Mothers and Deaf Preschool Children: Comparisons with Three Other Groups of Deaf and Hearing Dyads." *American Annals of the Deaf,* June 1981, pp. 454–468.

Peterson, C. C., and Siegal, M. "Deafness, Conversation and Theory of Mind." *Journal of Child Psychology and Psychiatry,* 1995, *36,* 459–474.

Peterson, C. C., and Siegal, M. "Changing Focus on the Representational Mind: Concepts of False Photos, False Drawings and False Beliefs in Deaf, Autistic and Normal Children." Unpublished manuscript, University of Queensland, Brisbane, Australia, 1997.

Power, D., and Carty, B. "Cross-Cultural Communication and the Deaf Community in Aus-tralia." In C. Hendrick and R. Holton (eds.), *Cross-Cultural Communication and Profes-sional Education.* Adelaide, South Australia: Flinders University Centre for Multicultural Studies, 1990.

Reed, T., and Peterson, C. C. "A Comparative Study of Autistic Subjects' Performance at Two Levels of Visual and Cognitive Perspective Taking." *Journal of Autism and Develop-mental Disorders,* 1990, *20,* 555–567.

Siddons, F., Happe, F., Whyte, R., and Frith, U. "Theory of Mind in Everyday Life: An Interview-Based Study with Autistic, Retarded and Disturbed Children." Paper pre-sented at the European Conference on Developmental Psychology, Stirling Univer-sity, Great Britain, August 1990.

Siegal, M. *Knowing Children: Experiment in Conversation and Cognition.* (2nd ed.) Hove, Eng-land: Psychology Press, 1997.

Siegal, M., and Beattie, K. "Where to Look First for Children's Understanding of False Beliefs." *Cognition,* 1991, *38,* 1–12.

Siegal, M., and Peterson, C. C. "Children's Theory of Mind and the Conversational Terri-tory of Cognitive Development." In C. Lewis and P. Mitchell (eds.), *Origins of an Under-standing Mind.* Hillsdale, N.J.: Erlbaum, 1994.

Solomon, G., Johnson, S., Zaitchik, D., and Carey, S. "Like Father Like Son: Young Chil-dren's Understanding of How and Why Offspring Resemble Their Parents." *Child Devel-opment,* 1996, *67,* 151–171.

Springer, K., and Keil, F. "On the Development of Biologically Specific Beliefs: The Case of Inheritance." *Developmental Psychology,* 1989, *30,* 864–868.

Tager-Flusberg, H. "Autistic Children's Talk About Psychological States: Deficits in the Early Acquisition of a Theory of Mind." *Child Development,* 1992, *63,* 161–172.

Tager-Flusberg, H. "What Language Reveals About the Understanding of Minds in Children with Autism." In S. Baron-Cohen and others (eds.), *Understanding Other Minds.* Oxford, England: Oxford University Press, 1993.

Wellman, H. M., and Gelman, S. A. "Cognitive Development: Foundational Theories of Core Domains." *Annual Review of Psychology,* 1992, *43,* 337–375.

Zaitchik, D. "When Representations Conflict with Reality." *Cognition,* 1990, *35,* 41–68.

CANDIDA C. PETERSON and MICHAEL SIEGAL are readers in psychology at the Uni-versity of Queensland, Brisbane, Australia.

Naive psychology, physics, and biology are early-emerging core domains of thought in the sense that they are specialized learning mechanisms, influenced by both innate and sociocultural constraints.

Commentary: Core Domains of Thought, Innate Constraints, and Sociocultural Contexts

Giyoo Hatano

As the editors of this sourcebook have indicated, a growing number of researchers on conceptual development have argued that even young children possess differentiated understandings of important aspects of the world, especially psychological, biological, and physical phenomena. In other words, young children have already acquired autonomous core domains of thought: naive physics, naive biology, and naive psychology (or theory of mind). This argument for early understandings leads to the question "How early?" A majority of researchers now agree that children six years of age and older possess these core domains of thought. But what of four- and five-year-old children? If these core domains can be recognized among four- and five-year-olds, then what about three-year-olds? The argument also leads to several interesting theoretical questions about the nature of the core domains. What makes differentiated understandings possible so early? Are these domains differentiated early in life in all cultures? What kinds of cognitive constraints help children acquire these understandings? Are these constraints innate? What are the experiential bases for the early differentiation? The four preceding chapters in this sourcebook have offered intriguing ideas as well as data to answer these questions. In this chapter I focus on three issues emerging from their contributions.

Do Young Children Possess Core Domains of Thought?

First, do young children possess what might properly be called naive theories of the world? Do they not only reveal different types of causal reasoning but also use them in flexible and appropriate ways? As alluded to by the editors, it is not particularly surprising that young children can divide entities into a few ontological classes and explain the behaviors of typical members of a few contrasting classes in different ways. Through interactions with other people, young children surely know that human behaviors are usually intentional; that is, they are based on desires and beliefs. Also, through experiences with acting on and receiving feedback from nonliving solid objects like stones, young children know that these objects stand still and stay unchanged unless external agents operate on them. It is rather straightforward to explain behaviors of other people in terms of their intentions, and behaviors of nonliving objects in terms of forces exerted from outside.

The task of classifying entities is more complicated in actuality, however, because there are many entities, varied in appearances, in between humans and nonliving entities: those that have agency but not transparent intentions (animals), those that spontaneously change but do not move around (plants), those that sometimes do something but only as the result of human agency (tools and machines), and others (including nonterrestrial objects and phenomena that seem to be entities). How to classify them or explain their behaviors is not as clear as in the case of humans or nonliving solid objects. However, it is still possible to categorize them and to apply some kinds of causality (such as teleological or vitalistic explanations) based on the classification.

The real complexity in developing such explanations lies in applying different types of causal reasoning to different behaviors by the same entities. As pointed out by Wellman, Hickling, and Schult in Chapter One, since humans are biological organisms, some of their behaviors must be understood in terms of the need to sustain life, either of the individual or of the species. That is, human behavior must be understood partly from a biological perspective. Animals (including humans) and plants are also physical entities, however, and so some of their behaviors should be explained in terms of the general laws of physics. In short, different types of causal devices have to be chosen for the same entities, depending on the nature of the behaviors being categorized.

The findings by Wellman, Hickling, and Schult are especially interesting and informative because they concentrate on children's explanations of human movements and actions that might induce psychological, physical, or biological reasoning. They take up young children's explanations of contrasting phenomena, both in the laboratory and in everyday life, and examine whether young children can apply types of causal reasoning that best fit the target phenomena. They found that "children evidence at least three basic everyday reasoning systems as early as two years of age—physical and psychological reasoning surely, and even biological reasoning in a rudimentary form"—and apply them in flexible and sensible ways.

However, it is premature to conclude that children as young as two or three possess naive psychology, physics, and biology. The laboratory data provided by Wellman, Hickling, and Schult clearly show that even three-year-olds differentiate between psychology and physics; but as the authors hint in their final discussion, the data are not conclusive for children's understanding of biology, which is probably the hardest domain of thought to differentiate among the three. Their three-year-olds gave as many psychological explanations as biological ones for the biological story. Their natural language analyses demonstrate that two- and three-year-olds offer very different patterns of explanation for human behavior versus that of physical objects, but their data are not very informative regarding children's explanations of other living things, including plants.

Inagaki's results, reported in Chapter Two, strongly suggest that differentiating between biology and psychology may take longer than two or three years after birth. Although she concludes that preschool children distinguish biological phenomena from psychological ones in their causal reasoning, she also points out that their reasoning about biological phenomena is sometimes influenced by social or psychological variables, especially when these variables are salient or biological variables are not explicitly indicated. For example, although her three-year-olds correctly recognized that internal bodily functions such as heartbeat and respiration are less controllable than hunger or thirst, they overestimated the mind's ability to control these internal bodily phenomena. Moreover, the children regarded biological (that is, nutritional) factors as more important than social or psychological factors in reducing disease transmission, but they did not regard social or psychological factors as negligible in this regard.

These results suggest that although three-year-olds have surely acquired naive physics and psychology, it is still debatable whether they have developed a biological domain of thought that includes humans, nonhuman animals, and plants; whether they possess a uniquely biological mode of reasoning; and, if they do possess such a mode, whether they always apply it to biological phenomena, such as nutrition, becoming ill, growth and death, and reproduction. Considering that for humans as a species it has been essential to have some knowledge about animals and plants as potential foods (Wellman and Gelman, 1992) and also to have knowledge about our bodily functions to maintain our health (Hatano, 1989), I am convinced that naive biology is one of the core domains. Whether it is acquired as early as the other two core domains is another issue, however. Whether naive biology is a distinct theory or mode of construal from the start (Keil, 1992) constitutes another question.

It is true that there are several reasons to believe that humans construct a domain of biology quite early and possess a distinct naive biology from the beginning. The natural classification scheme of the human mind (Atran, 1995), which categorizes entities into humans, nonhuman animals, plants, and nonliving things, seems to serve as a basis for naive biology. Skeletal principles differentiating between animate and inanimate entities (Gelman, 1990), and abstract knowledge assuming different insides for natural kinds versus artifacts (Simons and Keil, 1995), also seem to contribute to the early construction of a naive biology, because they are taken for granted before a large amount of factual knowledge has been accumulated.

However, an autonomous domain of biology (or a causal-explanatory framework unique for biological properties and processes) may be established later than naive psychology and naive physics, for several reasons. Understanding bodily processes, an essential component of naive biology, may be delayed, because it presupposes an *awareness* of the processes, as indicated by Inagaki. A biological mode of causal reasoning may be harder to acquire because it is neither intentional nor mechanical in nature. It also requires the construction of an integrated category of living things, including animals and plants, which have a very dissimilar appearance.

How Innate Constraints Work

Like most, if not all, of the other contributors to this sourcebook, I assume that the core domains of thought are also privileged domains (Siegler and Crowley, 1994) or innate domains (Carey, 1995). In other words, if a knowledge system deals with aspects of the world that are important for the survival of the human species and is thus shared by most adults both within and between cultures, I expect that humans are endowed with domain-specific principles and constraints for acquiring that knowledge system and that it is thus acquired early in life and without difficulty. (By the term *principle* here I mean only a set of similar constraints, biases, or tendencies, not a propositional form of knowledge.) As Atran (1994, p. 318) aptly put it, such "core" domains of human knowledge seem to operate under severe cognitive constraints. Early-differentiated understandings of important aspects of the world—the central claim of this sourcebook as a whole—are the best evidence for the assumption that the core domains are privileged, because it is highly unlikely that the domains can be differentiated so early just by domain-general learning mechanisms.

I also assume, like most of the other contributors to this sourcebook, that these three core domains of thought constitute theories. According to Carey (1995), a theory determines a range of phenomena that it is properly applied to; the theory also provides modes of explanation for the phenomena in its domain. Thus the domain-specific constraints mentioned above should enable young children not only to choose proper phenomena but also to induce a basic form of causal explanation of the domain.

As alluded to in the opening paragraph of the Editors' Notes, each core domain of thought probably emerges as a framework for predicting and interpreting typical "behaviors" of the objects covered by it—in the case of naive physics, the motion of inanimate, solid objects; in the case of naive psychology, the social activity of humans. It may be the case that human infants or toddlers possess a few distinct modes of causal reasoning, and each of them serves as the basis of a core domain of thought—only those objects that tend to reveal behaviors that can be readily explained by the particular mode of causal reasoning are incorporated into the domain. Alternatively, it may also be the case that entities are first grouped into several ontological and other domains in terms of their similarities, and then the domain-general mechanism of causal reasoning (for example, identifying causal devices from the pattern of covariations, Cheng, forthcoming), focusing on those entities of the domain, produces a domain-specific mode of causal reasoning. Naive theories develop further by providing children with reasonable hypotheses for observed phenomena.

Thus, innate constraints operating in the core domains should serve to control and direct attention or coding and restrict the range of hypothesis space to be explored. A unique set of constraints in each core domain draws attention to relevant aspects of the target objects or phenomena so that even young children can distinguish those that should be interpreted within the domain from those that should not. In the case of naive biology, for example, there seem to be a set of constraints directing attention to those aspects of living things that serve to distinguish them from nonliving things. For example, we now know that even infants can differentiate animals (including humans) that spontaneously move from inanimate entities that do not move by themselves. By age three or four, children are able to predict whether a given object can move up a hill by itself, disregarding its physical appearance (Massey and Gelman, 1988).

Another set of constraints serves to eliminate in advance a large number of logically possible interpretations or hypotheses. Again, an example from naive biology might clarify this point. As Garcia (1981) demonstrated for the first time, even rats tend to attribute bodily disturbances to novel food they have eaten. It seems likely that humans are endowed with similar constraints—trying to find the cause from among a variety of foods for a case of diarrhea or seeking a physical cause for a cut. In other words, it is assumed that because humans' tendencies and biases in our searches for interpretations enable us to explore the hypothesis space highly selectively, we can reach, in most cases, a reasonable interpretation promptly and thus can accumulate pieces of knowledge to form a core domain of thought.

However, these constraints may seldom take the form of specific knowledge. They can best be described as general, abstract principles that merely guide the acquisition of more specific (and immediately useful) pieces of knowledge through concrete experiences. This is probably because, in terms of natural selection, possessing specific pieces of information may actually be highly detrimental when the environment changes. For example, even if humans are endowed with a few principles of naive biology, as asserted by Inagaki, such principles can be applied only after children have learned what in their environment belongs to the category of living things.

Integrating Innate and Sociocultural Constraints

The notion of innate constraints does not exclude the possibility that sociocultural constraints operate simultaneously and significantly on the development of core domains of understanding. Carey (1995, p. 303), in answering a question, indicated that "innate domains are learning mechanisms," and thus "to characterize an innate domain one must characterize the precise role of experience."

It is sometimes claimed that, either explicitly or implicitly, because conceptual development is constrained by innate or early cognitive tendencies that are supposed to be more or less universal, the development itself must be more or less uniform, especially at early ages. The contribution of the surrounding environment of a growing child and her or his experience within it has often been assumed to be negligible or to merely facilitate or inhibit a fixed course of conceptual development. It is also claimed that although children's experience is critical in actualizing conceptual development, what makes the greatest difference is not specific experiences provided by the culture but rather the amount of general experience of acting on the environment and receiving feedback from it, which can neatly be approximated by children's age.

Neither of the above justifications is acceptable. To refute them I would like to emphasize that innate constraints are skeletal (Gelman, 1990) though strong, whereas sociocultural ones are specified though weak. Naive theories about the target aspect of the world share some basic, cognitive features in a variety of cultures, but at the same time they are instantiated differently according to those cultures. Because innate principles are too skeletal to be called a theory and thus have to be instantiated by a variety of sociocultural constraints, even initial forms of theories are likely to differ across cultures. Learning mechanisms need specific experiences for them to operate.

I think Peterson and Siegal's results, reported in Chapter Four, are particularly intriguing because they reveal a specific experiential variable that affects the selected core domains. Their data replicate the clear dissociation between psychological and physical understandings among autistic children reported by, among others, Baron-Cohen (1995). However, Peterson and Siegal present evidence for deaf individuals' similarly delayed development in psychological reasoning. More interestingly, their data showed that deaf children raised by hearing parents, and thus without fluent signing conversational interaction, had selective deficits in psychological reasoning, whereas deaf children from families with a fluent signer did not show such deficits. These results led the authors to legitimately emphasize the significance of conversational experience with a significant other in the development of naive psychological understanding.

I do not deny that differentiation among the core domains is "hardwired" in human beings. It may be due to special systems designed to construe different phenomena. In a neuroimaging study Fletcher and others (1995) found that stories requiring theory of mind to understand activated a specific area of the brain that stories consisting of physical sequences of events (but involving a human protagonist) did not activate. It seems plausible that, as the editors of this sourcebook have indicated, these brain systems might be impaired in some individuals and that autistic individuals are indeed impaired, for genetic reasons, in the development of normal brain systems supporting naive psychological reasoning and understanding. In Chapter Three Baron-Cohen argues along these lines and discusses his massive and intriguing data that clearly show autistic children's selective impairment in naive psychology. The data also show that autistic children are normal or even above normal in their capacity to deal with aspects of the world that do not involve intentionality. He provides new data showing that fathers and grandfathers of autistic children are engineers at a much higher rate than among the general population. It is strongly suggested that autistic individuals have inherited, at least to some extent, this clear dissociation between naive physics and naive psychology.

Although the editors seem to oppose nativistic and experiential accounts of a specific deficiency when they indicate that Peterson and Siegal's study alludes to the possibility of characterizing all these domains as being based on the accumulation of expertise, I strongly believe that Peterson and Siegal's results are completely compatible with the assumption of a theory of mind as an innate domain. As Carey (1995) said, "innate domains are learning mechanisms," and therefore the assumption of a theory of mind as an innate domain requires experience for the theory to emerge and develop.

References

Atran, S. "Core Domains Versus Scientific Theories: Evidence from Systematics and Itza-Maya Folkbiology." In L. A. Hirschfeld and S. A. Gelman (eds.), *Mapping the Mind: Domain Specificity in Cognition and Culture.* Cambridge, England: Cambridge University Press, 1994.

Atran, S. "Causal Constraints on Categories and Categorical Constraints on Biological Reasoning Across Cultures." In D. Sperber, D. Premack, and A. J. Premack (eds.), *Causal Cognition: A Multi-disciplinary Debate.* New York: Oxford University Press, 1995.

Baron-Cohen, S. *Mindblindness: An Essay on Autism and Theory of Mind.* Cambridge, Mass.: Bradford Books, 1995.

Carey, S. "On the Origin of Causal Understanding." In D. Sperber, D. Premack, and A. J. Premack (eds.), *Causal Cognition: A Multi-disciplinary Debate.* New York: Oxford University Press, 1995.

Cheng, P. W. "From Covariation to Causation: A Causal Power Theory." *Psychological Review,* forthcoming.

Fletcher, P. C., and others. "Other Minds in the Brain: A Functional Imaging Study of 'Theory of Mind' in Story Comprehension." *Cognition,* 1995, 57, 109–128.

Garcia, J. "Tilting at the Paper Mills of Academe." *American Psychologist,* 1981, 36, 149–158.

Gelman, R. "First Principles Organize Attention to and Learning About Relevant Data: Number and the Animate-Inanimate Distinction as Examples." *Cognitive Science,* 1990, 14, 79–106.

Hatano, G. "Language Is Not the Only Universal Knowledge System: A View from 'Everyday Cognition.' " *Dokkyo Studies in Data Processing and Computer Science,* 1989, 7, 69–76.

Keil, F. C. "The Origins of an Autonomous Biology." In M. Gunnar and M. Maratsos (eds.), *Minnesota Symposia on Child Psychology,* Vol. 25: *Modularity and Constraints in Language and Cognition.* Hillsdale, N.J.: Erlbaum, 1992.

Massey, C. M., and Gelman, R. "Preschoolers' Ability to Decide Whether a Photographed Unfamiliar Object Can Move Itself." *Developmental Psychology,* 1988, 24, 307–317.

Siegler, R. S., and Crowley, K. "Constraints on Learning in Nonprivileged Domains." *Cognitive Psychology,* 1994, *27,* 194–226.

Simons, D. J., and Keil, F. C. "An Abstract to Concrete Shift in the Development of Biological Thought: The *Insides* Story." *Cognition,* 1995, *56,* 129–163.

Wellman, H. M., and Gelman, S. A. "Cognitive Development: Foundational Theories of Core Domains." *Annual Review of Psychology,* 1992, *43,* 337–375.

GIYOO HATANO is professor of human relations at Keio University, Tokyo.

INDEX

Asperger Syndrome (AS), 50. *See also* Autism
Astington, J. W., 2, 56, 58
Atran, S., 2, 23, 28, 73, 74, 75
Autism: concepts-of-mind deficit in, 56; executive dysfunction theory of, 52; folk psychology/physics and, 47, 52; genetic-based brain impairment and, 51–52; male brain and, 51; mindblindness and, 52; modes of causal cognition and, 52; neurological damage and, 56; obsession and, 52; occupation and, 50–51; repetitive behavior and, 52; theory-of-mind account of, 52
Autistic adults: Embedded Figures Test and, 50; as engineers, 50–51, 77; folk physics and, 50–51
Autistic children: conversational deficit of, 56; deaf children and, 56; false-belief tasks and, 49, 56, 58, 61, 66–67; folk psychology deficit of, 46; mechanical obsession of, 47–48; naive psychology and, 77; psychological reasoning in, 4; social aloofness of, 56; theory of mind and, 56. *See also* Children's knowledge domains and conversational deficit (study)
Autistic children, folk physics and: anecdotal evidence and, 47–48; animate-inanimate distinction and, 50; autistic adults' folk psychology and, 50–51; brain function study and, 49–50; experimental evidence and, 49–50; false-belief study and, 49; false-photo study and, 49; family study evidence and, 50–51; genetics and, 51; object permanence and, 50
Autonomous biological domain: debate about, 27; emergence of, 28–31, 42–43, 74. *See also* Biological understanding; Domains, of knowledge; Naive biology

Backscheider, A. G., 8, 28
Bailey, S., 50
Baillargeon, R., 2, 23, 46
Banarjee, M., 9
Baron-Cohen, S., 2, 45, 46, 47, 49, 50, 51, 52, 56, 59, 61, 66, 75

Beattie, K., 57, 58, 67
Berlin, D., 68
Bettelheim, B., 47
Bibace, R., 38
Biological understanding: acquisition of, 1–2; causal reasoning and, 74; causal-explanatory framework for, 30; children's explanations and, 11–14, 17, 19–23; as core domain, 73; cross-cultural stability of, 68–69; debate about, 23; domain-specific development of, 29; early development of, 29, 42–43; emergence of, 28; guiding principles of, 30; of human behavior, 72; as outgrowth of physical understanding, 28–29; as outgrowth of psychological understanding, 29–30; research on, 2; uniqueness of, 23. *See also* Autonomous biological domain; Children's biological understanding; Children's understanding of illness (studies); Mind-body distinction, in children (studies); Naive biology
Biro, S., 46
Bishop, J., 64
Bloom, L., 15, 23
Bolton, P., 50
Brain: as causation-focused cognitive machine, 51; modes of causal cognition in, 52
Brentano, D. von, 46
Brown, J. R., 57, 67
Bullock, M., 2, 23, 28

Carey, S., 2, 3, 4, 9, 23, 27, 29, 31, 45, 47, 68, 74, 76
Carlson, V., 28
Carmichael, H., 57
Carty, B., 56
Causal cognition, 46
Causal reasoning: biological mode of, 74; children's explanations and, 7–8, 13, 72; classifying entities and, 72
Causal-explanatory framework of knowledge, 7–8, 13, 30, 74
Charman, T., 49
Charrow, V., 67
Cheng, P. W., 75

79

Child Language Data Exchange System (CHILDES), 15
Children: causal reasoning by, 72; classification of entities of, 72; cognitive development of, 1, 55; coherent bodies of, 27; domains of thought of, 71–74; emergence of mind-body distinction in, 31–38; naive theories of, 27; worldview of, 1. *See also* Autistic children; Children's explanations; Children's knowledge domains and conversational deficit (study); Children's understanding; Children's understanding of illness (studies); Infants; Knowledge, children's; Mind-body distinction, children's (studies); Thinking, children's
Children's biological understanding: early emergence of, 29; nutriment intake and, 30; personification and, 31; somatosensation and, 31. *See also* Children's understanding of illness (studies); Mind-body distinction, in children (studies); Naive biology
Children's explanations: behavioral, 17; biological, 11, 17, 19–23; of biologically impossible actions, 13–14; categories of, 11, 16–17; causal basis of, 7–8, 13, 72; of desired actions, 13–15; eliciting, 11; in everyday situations, 15; explanation modes and, 16–17, 19–20; explanation offers and, 17–20; explanation requests and, 18–19; explanation topics and, 16, 18–19; of human behavior, 8–10, 20–23; of human vs. object behavior, 20–22; of mistakes, 10, 13; natural language analyses and, 15–22; physical, 11, 17, 19–23; of physically impossible actions, 13–14; of possible actions, 13–14; psychological, 9, 11, 15, 17, 19–23; recent studies of, 10–15; researching, 23–24; simple uses and, 18; of story types, 11–13; syntactic dimensions in, 16; theories about, 9
Children's knowledge domains and conversational deficit (study): aims of, 57–58; animal biology task and, 62–63; autistic, deaf, and normal individuals (study), 57–69; background, 56–57; biological understanding and, 64–65; conclusions, 66–69; experimental tasks, 61–63; false photographic representation and, 64; false-belief task and, 58, 61, 66–67; false-photo task and, 58, 61–62, 68; interdo-

main associations and, 65–66; methods/procedures, 59–63; persistence of species characteristics and, 65; predictions, 59; results, 63–66; seed biology task and, 62; species characteristics tasks and, 59, 62–63; theory of mind and, 63–64. *See also* Domains, of thought
Children's understanding: of biological phenomena, 2, 4; of biology, 73; folk theories and, 3–4; of physical world, 2, 4; of physics, 72–73; of psychological realm, 2, 4; of psychology, 72–73; research on, 2. *See also* Children's explanations; Children's understanding of illness (studies); Mind-body distinction, children's (studies); Thinking, children's; *and by specific domain*
Children's understanding, of illness (studies): biological vs. social/psychological factors and, 40–41; bodily resistance to illness and, 38–39; exogenous factors and, 38; traditional beliefs and, 38
Classification of entities, 72
Cognitive development: of children, 1, 55; constraints and, 76; conversation and, 57; knowledge acquisition and, 1; questions about, 1. *See also* Children's knowledge domains and conversational deficit (study)
Cognitive modules, 4
Cohen, D.; 45
Constraints: on cognitive development, 76; functions of, 75; integrating innate and sociocultural, 75–77; of knowledge domains, 74–75; operation of, 75; as specific knowledge, 75
Conversation: autistic children and family, 56; cognitive development and, 57, 67; deaf children and family, 56–57, 67, 69; theory of mind and, 69. *See also* Children's knowledge domains and conversational deficit (study)
Crowley, K., 74

Deaf children: autistic children and, 56; false-belief tasks and, 58, 61, 66–67; family conversation and, 56–57, 66–67; mental-state references of, 57, 67; psychological reasoning of, 5, 76; in signing vs. hearing families, 56–58, 66–67; theory of mind and, 56. *See also* Children's knowledge domains and conversational deficit (study)

Deleau, M., 56, 66
Dennett, D., 45, 46
Domains, of knowledge: accumulation of expertise and, 77; cognitive development and, 1, 55; constraints of, 74–75; core, 74; differentiation among, 76; early understanding of, 2; everyday theories and, 3–4; gradual differentiation of, 3; innate conceptions of, 3; interconnection of, 2; research on, 2; theory of mind and, 77. *See also* Autonomous biological domain; Children's knowledge domains and conversational deficit (study); *and by specific domain*
Domains, of thought: cognitive modules and, 4; cross-comparative research on, 2; early acquisition of, 71; as privileged, 74; principles and, 74
Donelan-McCall, N., 57
Down's syndrome children, 56, 67
Dunn, J., 57, 67

Embedded Figures Test, 50
Erting, C., 57
Estes, D., 8
Executive dysfunction theory, 52
Explanandum, 16
Explanans, 16–17
Explanation modes, 16–17, 19–20
Explanation offer, 18–20
Explanation request, 18–19
Explanation topics, 16, 18–19
Explanations: biological, 11, 17, 19–23; defining, 7; of human behavior, 8–10, 20; physical, 11, 17, 19–23; psychological, 9, 11, 17, 19–23. *See also* Children's explanations

False-belief task, 49, 56, 58, 61, 66–67
False-photo task, 49, 58, 61–62, 68
Farnham, J., 52
Fletcher, J., 67
Fletcher, P. C., 4, 75
Folk physics: adaptive function of, 51; animate-inanimate distinction and, 46; autistic adults and, 50–51; autistic children and, 47–51; causal cognition and, 46–47; defined, 46; emergence of, 46; folk psychology and, 46; hominid evolution and, 52. *See also* Naive physics
Folk psychology: adaptive function of, 51; autistic adults and, 50–51; causal cognition and, 46–47; deficit of, in autistic

children, 46; defined, 45; emergence of, 46; folk physics and, 46. *See also* Mentalizing; Naive psychology; Theory of mind
Folk theories, 3–4. *See also* Naive theories of knowledge
Folstein, S., 50
Frith, U., 45, 49, 50, 56, 61, 66

Garcia, J., 75
Gelman, R., 2, 8, 23, 28, 73, 75
Gelman, S. A., 8, 22, 23, 27, 28, 55, 58, 62, 65, 73, 75
Gergely, C., 46
Gergely, G., 46
Golinkoff, R. M., 28
Goodhart, F., 45
Greenberg, M. T., 57
Gregory, S., 64
Gutheil, G., 43

Halpern, J., 51
Hammer, J., 50, 51
Happe, F., 56
Harding, C. G., 28
Harris, P. L., 2
Hart, C., 47
Hatano, G., 2, 8, 28, 29, 30, 31, 32, 73
Heider, F., 45
Hickling, A. K., 15
Hood, L., 15, 23
Human behavior: biological perspective on, 72; children's explanations of, 8–10, 20–23; explanations of, 8–10, 20; social aspect of, 1

Illness. *See* Children's understanding of illness (studies)
Inagaki, K., 2, 8, 28, 30, 31, 32, 59, 67
Infants: biological knowledge and, 28; intentionality detector and, 47; physical understanding of, 23. *See also* Children
Innate constraints, 74–76. *See also* Constraints
Intentionality detector, 47

Jenkins, J. M., 57
Johnson, C. N., 8
Johnson, S., 68
Jolliffe, T., 50

Kalish, C. W., 2, 8, 22, 28, 38
Keeble, S., 46, 47

Keil, F. C., 2, 22, 28, 29, 31, 43, 58, 73
Kister, M. C., 38
Knowledge: adults' vs. children's, 1. *See also* Children's understanding; Domains, of knowledge
Knowledge acquisition: folk theories and, 1–2. *See also* Domains, of knowledge
Kotovsky, L., 2, 8, 46
Kremer, K. E., 8, 28

Laudan, L., 4
Le Couteur, A., 50
Leekam, S., 49
Legerstee, M., 8
Leslie, A. M., 45, 46, 47, 49, 56, 58, 61, 66, 67
Lovell, A., 47

MacWhinney, B., 15
Male brain, 31
Marschark, M., 67
Massey, C. M., 28, 75
McCormick, M., 2, 8, 28
Meadow, K. P., 57, 67
Meck, E., 8
Mental retardation: theory of mind and, 56. *See also* Down's syndrome children
Mentalizing: defined, 45; studies of, 45–46
Mind: adaptability and evolution of, 51; natural classification scheme of, 73
Mind-body distinction, in children (studies): emergence of, 31–38; in four- and five-year-olds, 31–32; mind's inability to control bodily processes and, 32–34; mind's inability to control stomach processes and, 34–38; in three- and four-year-olds, 34–38; in three-to-five-year-olds, 32–34
Mortimore, C., 50
Morton, J., 45
Mundy, P., 50

Nadasdy, Z., 46
Naive biology: early acquisition of, 73; early emergence of, 29; early vs. later development of, 28, 42–43; innate constraints and, 75; naive physics/psychology and, 28, 42–43; native classification scheme and, 73. *See also* Biological understanding; Children's biological understanding
Naive physics: early development of,

27–28; naive biology and, 28, 42–43. *See also* Folk physics; Physical understanding
Naive psychology: autistic children and, 77; early development of, 27–28; naive biology and, 28, 42–43. *See also* Folk psychology; Psychological reasoning
Naive theories of knowledge, 27, 55–56, 68. *See also* Folk theories
Natural language analyses, 15–22
Needham, A., 2, 8, 46

Olson, D. R., 2
Ozonoff, S., 52

Patterson, C. J., 38
Pennington, B., 52
Perner, J., 2, 45, 49
Peterson, C. C., 2, 56, 57, 58, 59, 64, 66
Phillips, A. T., 8, 46
Physical understanding: acquisition of, 1–2; biological understanding as outgrowth of, 28–29; children's explanations and, 11–14, 17, 19–23; early development of, 22–23; of infants, 23; research on, 2. *See also* Folk physics; Naive physics
Piaget, J., 1, 8, 23
Pinker, S., 51
Power, D., 56
Premack, A. J., 46
Premack, D., 46, 47
Psychological reasoning: acquisition of, 1–2; in autistic individuals, 5; belief- and desire-based, 22–23; biological understanding as outgrowth of, 29–30; children's application of, 22–23; children's explanations and, 9, 11–14, 15, 17, 19–23; cross-domain comparative research and, 2; of deaf children, 76; in deaf individuals, 5; as default mode for children, 43; potential error in, 22–23. *See also* Naive psychology

Reasoning. *See* Domains, of thought; Psychological reasoning; Thinking, children's
Reed, T., 56
Robertson, M., 50
Rogers, S., 52
Rosengren, K. S., 2, 8, 28
Russell, J., 50, 52
Rutter, M., 50

Sardo, M., 9
Schult, C. A., 10
Sexton, M. E., 28
Shah, A., 50
Shatz, M., 8, 28
Sheldon, L., 64
Sherman, T., 50
Shultz, T. R., 2, 9
Siddons, F., 56
Siegal, M., 2, 38, 56, 57, 58, 59, 64, 66, 67
Siegler, R. S., 74
Sigman, M., 50
Simmel, M., 45
Simons, D. J., 28, 73
Smith, M. C., 9
Snow, C., 15
Sociocultural constraints, 75–76. See also Constraints
Solomon, G., 68
Spelke, E. S., 2, 8, 9, 23, 27, 46
Sperber, D., 46
Springer, K., 38, 58

Tager-Flusberg, H., 45, 56, 67
Thaiss, L., 49, 56, 58
Theory of bodies mechanism (ToBy), 47
Theory of mind: autism and, 52; autistic children and, 45, 56; children's knowledge domains (study), 63–64; conversation and, 69; deafness and, 56;
defined, 45; as innate knowledge domain, 77; intentionality detector and, 47; mechanisms of, 47; mental retardation and, 56; neurological vs. conversational account of, development, 57; research on, 2, 22–23. See also Folk psychology; Mentalizing
Theory of mind mechanism (ToMM), 47
Thinking. See Domains, of thought
Thinking, children's: causal-explanatory system of, 7–8; comparative studies of, 2, 8; entity-based theory of, 9, 22; late differentiation in, 1; Piaget's theory of, 1–2, 8–9. See also Children's understanding; Explanations, children's; and by specific domain

Ungerer, J., 50

Vera, A., 43

Walsh, M. E., 38
Wellman, H. M., 2, 4, 8, 9, 10, 15, 22, 23, 27, 55, 58, 62, 68, 73
Wells, D., 9
Whyte, R., 56
Wimmer, H., 45
Woodward, A. L., 8, 46
Woolley, J. D., 22

Zaitchik, D., 61, 68

Ordering Information

MAIL ORDERS TO:
Jossey-Bass Publishers
350 Sansome Street
San Francisco, California 94104-1342

PHONE subscription or single-copy orders toll-free at (888) 378-2537 or at (415) 433-1767 (toll call).

FAX orders toll-free to (800) 605-2665.

NEW DIRECTIONS FOR CHILD DEVELOPMENT is a series of paperback books that presents the latest research findings on all aspects of children's psychological development, including their cognitive, social, moral, and emotional growth. Books in the series are published quarterly in Fall, Winter, Spring, and Summer and are available for purchase by subscription and individually.

SUBSCRIPTIONS cost $65.00 for individuals (a savings of 35 percent over single-copy prices) and $105.00 for institutions, agencies, and libraries. Standing orders are accepted. New York residents, add local sales tax for subscriptions. (For subscriptions outside the United States, add $7.00 for shipping via surface mail or $25.00 for air mail. Orders *must be prepaid* in U.S. dollars by check drawn on a U.S. bank or charged to VISA, MasterCard, or American Express.)

SINGLE COPIES cost $25.00 plus shipping (see below) when payment accompanies order. California, New Jersey, New York, and Washington, D.C., residents, please include appropriate sales tax. Canadian residents, add GST and any local taxes. Billed orders will be charged shipping and handling. No billed shipments to post office boxes. (Orders from outside the United States *must be prepaid* in U.S. dollars by check drawn on a U.S. bank or charged to VISA, MasterCard, or American Express.)

SHIPPING (SINGLE COPIES ONLY): $30.00 and under, add $5.50; to $50.00, add $6.50; to $75.00, add $7.50; to $100.00, add $9.00; to $150.00, add $10.00.

ALL PRICES are subject to change.

DISCOUNTS FOR QUANTITY ORDERS are available. Please write to the address above for information.

ALL ORDERS must include either the name of an individual or an official purchase order number. Please submit your order as follows:
Subscriptions: specify series and year subscription is to begin
Single copies: include individual title code (such as CD59)

FOR SUBSCRIPTION SALES OUTSIDE OF THE UNITED STATES, contact any international subscription agency or Jossey-Bass directly.

OTHER TITLES AVAILABLE IN THE
NEW DIRECTIONS FOR CHILD DEVELOPMENT SERIES
William Damon, Editor-in-Chief

CD74 Understanding How Family-Level Dynamics Affect Children's Development:
Studies of Two-Parent Families, *James P. McHale, Philip A. Cowan*
CD73 Children's Autonomy, Social Competence, and Interactions with Adults and
Other Children: Exploring Connections and Consequences, *Melanie Killen*
CD72 Creativity from Childhood Through Adulthood: The Developmental Issues,
Mark A. Runco
CD71 Leaving Home: Understanding the Transition to Adulthood,
Julia A. Graber, Judith Semon Dubas
CD70 After the Wall: Family Adaptations in East and West Germany,
James Youniss
CD69 Exploring Young Children's Concepts of Self and Other Through
Conversation, *Linda L. Sperry, Patricia A. Smiley*
CD68 African American Family Life: Its Structural and Ecological Aspects,
Melvin N. Wilson
CD67 Cultural Practices as Contexts for Development, *Jacqueline J. Goodnow,
Peggy J. Miller, Frank Kessel*
CD66 Beliefs About Parenting: Origins and Developmental Implications,
Judith G. Smetana
CD65 Childhood Gender Segregation: Causes and Consequences,
Campbell Leaper
CD64 Children, Youth, and Suicide: Developmental Perspectives,
Gil G. Noam, Sophie Borst
CD63 Promoting Community-Based Programs for Socialization and Learning,
Francisco A. Villarruel, Richard M. Lerner
CD62 Father-Adolescent Relationships, *Shmuel Shulman, W. Andrew Collins*
CD61 The Development of Literacy Through Social Interaction, *Colette Daiute*
CD60 Close Friendships in Adolescence, *Brett Laursen*
CD59 The Role of Play in the Development of Thought, *Marc H. Bornstein,
Anne Watson O'Reilly*
CD58 Interpretive Approaches to Children's Socialization, *William A. Corsaro,
Peggy J. Miller*
CD57 Beyond the Parent: The Role of Other Adults in Children's Lives
Robert C. Pianta
CD56 The Development of Political Understanding: A New Perspective,
Helen Haste, Judith Torney-Purta
CD55 Emotion and Its Regulation in Early Development, *Nancy Eisenberg,
Richard A. Fabes*
CD54 Narrative and Storytelling: Implications for Understanding Moral
Development, *Mark B. Tappan, Martin J. Packer*
CD53 Academic Instruction in Early Childhood: Challenge or Pressure?
Leslie Rescorla, Marion C. Hyson, Kathy Hirsh-Pasek
CD52 Religious Development in Childhood and Adolescence, *Fritz K. Oser,
W. George Scarlett*
CD51 Shared Views in the Family During Adolescence, *Roberta L. Paikoff*
CD49 Child Care and Maternal Employment: A Social Ecology Approach,
Kathleen McCartney
CD48 Children's Perspectives on the Family, *Inge Bretherton, Malcolm W. Watson*
CD47 The Legacy of Lawrence Kohlberg, *Dawn Schrader*
CD46 Economic Stress: Effects on Family Life and Child Development,
Vonnie C. McLoyd, Constance Flanagan
CD45 Infant Stress and Coping, *Michael Lewis, John Worobey*
CD42 Black Children and Poverty: A Developmental Perspective, *Diana T. Slaughter*

CD40   Parental Behavior in Diverse Societies, *Robert A. LeVine, Patrice M. Miller,*
       Mary Maxwell West
CD39   Developmental Psychopathology and Its Treatment, *Ellen D. Nannis,*
       Philip A. Cowan
CD37   Adolescent Social Behavior and Health, *Charles E. Irwin, Jr.*

DATE DUE

DEC 2 1 '99			

GAYLORD   PRINTED IN U.S.A.

Jai Darlene

Jai Darlene is an army brat who traveled all over the world with her family before settling down in Fort Wayne, IN. She later moved to Indianapolis and obtained a juris doctorate from Indiana University School of Law, where she discovered an aptitude for writing, earning herself a spot on her school's Law Review. After practicing law for five years, Jai discovered her artistic talent through using her creative skills to litigate countless jury and bench trials. This inspired her to pursue her passion by harnessing her imagination to make fictional characters come to life.

Connect with Jai:
www.facebook.com/jaidarlene
www.twitter.com/jaibunni
www.instagram.com/jai_darlene

9 780985 351557